The Report
of the
Lutheran-Episcopal
Dialogue
Second Series
1976 — 1980

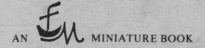

AN MINIATURE BOOK

© 1981 Forward Movement Publications, 412 Sycamore Street, Cincinnati, Ohio 45202. All rights reserved. Printed in U.S.A.   ISBN 0-88028-000-X

Contents

The History of the Lutheran-Episcopal Dialogue, Series Two

For more than a decade Lutherans and Episcopalians have been engaged in theological conversations in order to discover and to manifest more fully the unity given us by Jesus Christ. These conversations have taken place on the international, national and, to some degree, local levels.

The International Anglican-Lutheran Dialogue took place in four meetings between September of 1970 and April of 1972. "From the beginning these conversations sought to determine the conditions necessary for mutual recognition and fellowship between the two churches in the context of the mission of the church to the world. Such convergence and present agreement was found to exist in matters theological, liturgical, creedal, in sacramental life and practice, as well as to the place and role of the ordained ministry, that the conversations recommended a mutual recognition by Anglican and Lutheran churches seeing each other 'as a true communion of Christ's body possessing a truly apostolic ministry'."[1]

In the United States, representatives appointed by the then Joint Commission on Ecumenical Relations (JCER) of the Episcopal Church and the presidents of the Lutheran bodies in the Lutheran Council U.S.A. (LCUSA) met together in Dialogue I six times between October, 1969 and June, 1972. Although the objective laid down in the mandate to the participants was to "define the possibilities and problems for a more extended dialogue, having more specific fellowship or unity or union goals," Dialogue I went beyond that objective. "As we discussed the faith and the mission to which Christ calls us," they said, "we discovered both an existing unity and, in the face of massive cultural upheaval, an unavoidable imperative to manifest oneness."[2]

The Final Report of Dialogue I (Lutheran-Episcopal Dialogue: A Progress Report, 1973) submitted to the respective churches or agencies is divided into four parts: Preamble, Summary Statements developed from the first four meetings, Recommendations and Enabling Legislation. The report, published by Forward Movement, also included some of the theological papers considered by the Dialogue, a Report of the International Anglican-Lutheran Dialogue and a statement addressed to Lutherans and one addressed to Episcopalians by their respective representatives to the Dialogue team.

In the report the participants sought to make possible the practical implementation of mutual recognition by the Lutheran and Episcopal churches and local eucharistic intercommunion as soon as possible (pp. 22-24 Progress Report).

The Standing Commission on Ecumenical Relations of the Episcopal Church (then JCER) received the report of Dialogue I and recommended it to its Church for study. The desire for more historical and theological documentation prior to the implementation of the report's recommendations prompted the SCER to recommend further that a second series of Lutheran-Episcopal conversations be held.

On the Lutheran side, the report of Dialogue I was received by the Division of Theological Studies of LCUSA and transmitted to the three General Presidents of the participating churches for consideration. The report was received and the General Presidents authorized and appointed representatives to a second series of Lutheran-Episcopal conversations.

Accordingly, by request from the churches, Dialogue II of the Lutheran-Episcopal conversations began with a meeting at Virginia Theological Seminary in Alexandria, Virginia in January, 1976.

Lacking a detailed mandate for the objectives of Dialogue II, the participants picked up on recommendation IV-A-1 from the first series report, and the recommendation from the International Anglican-Lutheran Dialogue that continuing discussion be held on such topics as the proclamation of the gospel and the historic episcopate. Therefore, the agenda of the first session featured discussion papers on the topic, "What Is The Gospel?"

It remained for a subsequent meeting, however, to develop a common statement on the Gospel. The first meeting of our Dialogue II quickly focused on two questions that set the direction for our future conversations: 1) "What is our task?" and 2) "What has happened to the recommendations of Dialogue I?" In its own initial response to these questions the Dialogue drafted a resolution to the churches which generalized two agenda items for the second series of discussion: 1) "a further penetration of theological problems of concern to our churches" and 2) "encouraging and devising means of implementation for parish life." The participants also committed themselves in the same resolution to look toward mutual recognition of faith, ministry and sacraments and requested the churches to give more widespread consideration to the theological material of series one and to provide a formal response to its recommendations.

The response of the churches to our resolution did not evoke a clearer mandate for our work but it did encourage us to spell out more specifically our own goals for Dialogue II and to determine the theological questions which must be considered to assist in the attainment of these goals.

The members all came to the next meeting at Concordia Seminary, St Louis, in January, 1977, with their personal ideas and concerns for the purpose and content of our future meetings. These were shared and discussed with a mixture of enthusiasm and frustration. Some participants believed more dialogue on an academic level would prove fruitless until the churches took seriously the implementation of Report I; others held that theological studies and conversations are never altogether without purpose and that, especially in view of the fact that the U.S.A. is one of three places in the world (the others are Australia and Tanzania)[3] where Lutherans and Anglicans exist side by side in substantial numbers, we should continue. The general, though not unanimous, conclusion was stated as follows:

"The purpose of this second series of Lutheran-Episcopal Dialogues is to expand, clarify and contextualize for our churches the report of the first series: I - By clarifying the type of fellowship that has been proposed (Ecclesial Recognition, not Organic Union or full Intercommunion). II - By describing certain desirable results that the proposed recognition would make in church life. III - By considering the following subjects in papers prepared for sharing with local church members:

A. The History of Lutheran and Episcopalian Church Life in America;
B. Episcopacy, Apostolicity, The Gospel, and the role of the Bishop or pastoral *episcopē* in their churches;
C. Justification by Faith;

7

D. The Understanding of Christ's Eucharistic Presence;
E. How The Scripture is Authoritative for the Faith and Life of the Church;
F. Styles of Theological Reflection or Our Characteristic Ways of Doing Theology."

It was then projected that three more meetings, bringing the total to five sessions, would bring Dialogue II to the conclusion of its task. As we can now see, however, our ambition exceeded our ability and we soon found ourselves pressed to reach our goal in nine meetings.

The tempo of our schedule now increased from annual to semi-annual sessions and the next meeting was held at the University of the South in Sewanee, Tennessee, in September, 1977. Papers on the history of the Lutherans and Episcopalians in the U.S.A. and presentations on Episcopacy/Apostolicity were the main agenda items. Reactions and responses to an intermediate progress report from Dialogue II, however, indicated a need for both Lutherans and Episcopalians to examine Episcopacy/ Apostolicity and the Office of the Ministry at greater length. So, a number of additional assignments were made for subsequent meetings on "The Word *Apostolos* in the New Testament," "The Emergence of the Apostolicity Formula in the Early Church" and "Eucharistic Fellowship between Anglicans and European Lutherans."

The members of the Dialogue then requested copies of the documents presented at the International Lutheran-Anglican Dialogue in 1970-72, the 1965 issue of *Lutheran World* devoted to Anglican-Lutheran Encounter and Vol. 4 of Lutheran-Roman Catholic Dialogue containing an article on "A Lutheran View of Lutheran Orders." With the commitment to examine these materials individually and discuss them at a later meeting, the conclusion of our task was indeed moving farther into the future than we had envisioned.

Session four met in March, 1978, at Lutheran Theological Seminary (now Trinity) in Columbus, Ohio. It proved to be a signficiant milestone on the road to our objective. Following presentations on "Justification by Faith Alone" from members of the group, and a review of the "Malta Statement" from the Lutheran-Roman Catholic Dialogue, we drafted a common statement on Justification.

Encouraged by this positive action, we decided to aim for a joint statement on Apostolicity, if possible, at Nashotah House in September of the same year (1978). Still another paper was deemed important for this task, and to the list of those already assigned for the next session, one, on "Anglican Practice and Formularies Relating to Apostolicity," was added. At this time, too, and growing out of mutual concern to do our theological homework on all fronts, we elected to include presentations on "Proclamation of the Gospel" and "Faith and Baptism" on future agendas.

Session five at Nashotah House (September, 1978) generated the greatest optimism about future meetings of the Dialogue. While there, the finished LED Joint Statement on Justification was adopted (see below p. 22) and subsequently released for publication. The main topic "Apostle/Apostolicity," however, also uncovered wide areas of agreement between the Lutheran and Anglican traditions on the basis of New Testament, Patristic, and Reformation materials. Discussion on the historical development of the ordained ministry was very fruitful, and it was anticipated that at a future meeting of the Dialogue a joint statement on Apostolicity could be drafted. At this fifth session a representative of the

Association of Evangelical Lutheran Churches (AELC) also joined the Dialogue and remained a regular participant throughout the second series.

In November of 1978 the Episcopal Church held its first Ecumenical Consultation — an event designed to bring together participants from all of its several interchurch conversations and bilateral dialogues. From this Consultation emerged a statement on the Episcopal Church's vision of visible unity, subsequently adopted, with some emendations, at the 66th General Convention (Denver, September 1979). The Consultation also pressed for intensified dialogue with Lutherans and adopted a resolution of the 1978 Lambeth Conference as its own: (that Anglicans should) "give special attention to (the) ecclesial recognition of the Lutheran Church on the basis of reports and resolutions of the Anglican Consultative Council in Dublin (1973) and Trinidad (1976) as well as in the Pullach Report of 1972."[4]

Weather conditions across the country interfered with the sixth session meeting at Lutheran Southern Theological Seminary in Columbia, South Carolina, in January of 1979. Missed flight schedules and illness reduced the number of those attending the Dialogue making it impossible for the participants to draft any common statement. Useful and helpful discussion evolved, however, around the assigned subject on the Authority of Scripture within Anglicanism and Lutheranism. This session also devoted some time to discussing "A New Look at Apostolicity" produced by the (then) Joint Commission on Ecumenical Relations of the Episcopal Church in 1976 and introduced at the Nashotah meeting. From this sixth session there emerged the conviction on the part of all the participants that joint statements on the chief topics under study were not only possible but offered a fruitful means for progress in our Dialogue.

In August of the same year the members of the Dialogue assembled for their seventh session at Sewanee, Tennessee. The discussion which followed a paper on "The Authority of Scripture" by a Lutheran participant and the two papers on "The Eucharistic Presence" disclosed immense areas of agreement presently existing among the members of the Dialogue. Further exploration of the doctrine of ministry and ordination within Lutheranism produced additional data for the ongoing study of the subject of apostolicity and the historic episcopate. It was at this meeting that plans were crystalized for the end of the second series of the Dialogue within two or three more sessions and that drafting assignments for LED joint statements on Gospel, Authority of Scripture, Eucharistic Presence and Apostolicity were made.

The eighth session of the Dialogue (April, 1980, Concordia Theological Seminary, Ft. Wayne, Indiana) was planned as the final occasion for consideration of the remaining papers. The topics were: "The Theological Methodology of the Lutheran-Episcopal Dialogue," "How Lutherans Do Theology," "How Anglicans Do Theology," "Faith and Baptism," and "The Proclamation of The Gospel." The last two days were devoted to further discussion and the reworking of the proposed common statements.

The participants were able to adopt readily a joint statement on The Gospel; (see p. 24) minor changes were considered necessary in the draft on Eucharistic Presence, and some rewriting of the statement on Apostolocity was recommended. The preliminary statement on The Authority of Scripture was rejected and a new drafting committee was appointed to prepare a new version for the November meeting at Nashotah House.

Also, plans were drawn for the remaining task of completing the final report and the necessary recommendations coming from this second series of the Dialogue.

The ninth and final session of the second series of the Lutheran-Episcopal Dialogue was held at Nashotah House, Wisconsin, in November of 1980. Discussion centered on the remaining joint statements on Eucharistic Presence, Apostolicity, and Scripture. After textual changes were made in each of them, the Dialogue was able to adopt them as Joint Statements, (see pp. 25ff) thus completing one of the tasks set for this series in 1977. Further review of the paper on "The Theological Methodology of LED II" resulted in only minor emendations and it was unanimously adopted. The recommendations were studied, discussed and amended, but in the end two sets were proposed: a) the recommendations agreed upon by the Episcopal Church U.S.A., The American Lutheran Church, Association of Evangelical Lutheran Churches, and Lutheran Church in America participants; and b) the recommendations of the Lutheran Church-Missouri Synod participants.

As a final piece of business the Lutheran and Episcopalian participants each adopted a statement to their respective church memberships.

FOOTNOTES

1. Wright, J. R. (ed) *A Communion of Communions: One Eucharistic Fellowship,* (New York: Seabury, 1979) pp. 94f
2. *Lutheran-Episcopal Dialogue: A Progress Report,* (Cincinnati: Forward Movement Publications, 1973) p. 13
3. Information from Dan Martensen, Department of Studies, Lutheran World Federation, Geneva
4. *The Report of the Lambeth Conference,* (London: C10 Publishing, 1978) p. 49

2.
The Theological Methodology of LED II

The Genesis of LED II

The first series of Lutheran-Episcopal Dialogue produced what the participants regarded as sufficient doctrinal agreement between the two traditions to warrant the following steps subject to the approval of the appropriate authorities:

1. Mutual ecclesial recognition.
2. Encouragement of members of each denomination to feel free to receive the administrations of the other in appropriate circumstances.
3. Encouragement of local acts of intercommunion on appropriate occasion when a local congregation felt prepared for this step.

Two areas of theological concern which remain problems between the two communions were identified. These were:

1. (On the Lutheran side) The understanding of the nature of the gospel.
2. (On the Anglican side) The place of the historic episcopate.

It was felt that further dialogue on these questions should take place, but (and the participants attached great importance to this proviso) *only in the context of prior mutual ecclesial recognition and occasional eucharistic sharing.*

These suggestions and recommendations were forwarded to the appropriate organs of the respective church bodies. No implementing action, however, was taken. Instead, it was resolved by both parties that the dialogues should continue without ecclesial recognition and occasional eucharistic sharing. To some members of the LED I who were invited to continue the second series, this seemed a betrayal of the precondition for further dialogue which we had envisaged as *sine qua non*. One Lutheran participant subsequently withdrew from LED II while at least one member on the Episcopal side who had participated in LED I remained less than enthusiastic about the second series, put it low on his list of priorities, and attended only four sessions.

LED II, meeting under these somewhat discouraging circumstances, has nevertheless persevered in tackling the outstanding issues, (the nature of the gospel and apostolicity), plus other questions which have been put before us, either from within the dialogue or by our respective churches. These include: justification, the eucharist, and the authority of scripture.

The Joint Statement on Justification

The first topic to be concluded was the doctrine of justification. Rather early on (September, 1978) we were able to produce a joint statement on this doctrine. This statement, while not covering all that either side would have wished to say on the subject, especially the Lutherans, for whom it has been traditionally the *articulus stantis et cadentis ecclesiae,* represented those areas of the doctrine upon which we were able to make a joint statement.

The methodological implications of this momentous step are obvious, as will be seen from a paper prepared for the Detroit National Ecumenical Consultation of the Episcopal Church (November 1978) by Dr. William G. Rusch (Lutheran). First, Dr. Rusch made the pertinent remark that LED I went beyond its original mandate in making concrete proposals for mutual ecclesial recognition and limited intercommunion (Pulpit and altar fellowship or *communio in sacris).* Next in a report on the Lutheran World Federation's statement of attitude towards common negotiations he suggests that our present need is to move forward to joint confessional statements

14

in matters that have separated us. Such joint statements have a parallel in the ARCIC statements on Eucharist, Ministry and Authority. LED II's joint statement on justification might be seen as a model for just such a joint confession, if our respective churches could adopt the statement, recognize in it an expression of their own faith, and a basis for an essential "minimum agreement."

Apostolicity

On the subject of apostolicity and *episcopē* it obviously is not possible to make a joint statement covering all that Anglicans would want to say on the subject (any more than Lutherans would accept our joint statement on justification as their entire faith on that subject). Our statement, however, affirms such matters as:

1. That the ministry of word and sacraments is a gift of God "from above," not from the congregation "from below."

2. What Anglicans would call the "sacramental" character of ordination. (The word does not matter: it is the reality of ordination as an act of God the Spirit wrought through the laying on of hands and prayer).

3. Ministerial succession as one of the signs of the church's continuity from the apostles' time, and of its unity in space.

Some ancillary questions relating to the issue of the historic episcopate were put to the dialogue from the Standing Commission on Ecumenical Relations (of the Episcopal Church). One was, why had we not proposed that in interim eucharist fellowship we should practice concelebration, as in COCU? And a wider question, whether our proposed model of interim fellowship would be equally applicable to our relationship with other non-episcopal bodies (e.g., the COCU churches) with whom we are in dialogue?

On the narrower issue of concelebration, it was quickly discovered within the dialogue that such a practice would be foreign to Lutheran usage. And there was some sense that it looked suspiciously like a *sub rosa* attempt to legitimate or validate non-Episcopal ministrations despite lip-service to the reality of non-Episcopal ministries. While the Episcopalian members of the dialogue would maintain an episcopally ordained ministry as the only acceptable form of ministry within our own church, and would view it as essential in any organic reunion or full communion, we would not wish to recommend any practice that would show suspicion of the sacramental reality of present Lutheran administrations. Concelebration in itself might be harmless and even meaningful as an expression of some measure of already existing unity, yet when required as a precondition it would be contrary to the doctrine of ministry which we could in common affirm. So this model was rejected as a methodological framework for our dialogue. What the implication of this is for other dialogues in which the Episcopal church is involved is not for us to answer.

On the wider issue of the applicability of our model of limited altar and pulpit fellowship to interim relationships between the Episcopal church and other non-episcopal bodies, we would answer that our proposal of interim eucharistic sharing should be seen not in isolation, but in the context of the measure of doctrinal agreement affirmed in common statements of faith.

The Eucharist

Two other major issues were brought before the dialogue and have evoked papers from each side. The first was on the Eucharist. Both communions affirm the real presence of Christ's Body and Blood in the Lord's Supper, but they express this faith somewhat differently. Lutherans (especially strongly confessional Lutheranism

16

as represented by the Missouri Synod) tend to assert the Real Presence by doctrinal statement, as in the classical affirmations of *manducatio impiorum* and *manducatio oralis*. Although Article XXIX refers to these questions, and takes a somewhat different stand on them from that of classical Lutheranism, Anglicans today have no interest in these particular doctrinal affirmations. Rather, they tend to express their belief in the Real Presence in ceremonial action, by the reverence with which they treat the consecrated elements outside of Communion. The Book of Common Prayer requires that they either be reverently consumed after the Communion or reverently reserved for delayed Communion as on Maundy Thursday for Good Friday. Further, there is the issue of the eucharistic sacrifice. Lutheranism has generally been shy of any sacrificial element in the eucharist except the secondary offerings such as alms (bread and wine?), prayers, praise, etc. There is a strong stream of thought in Anglicanism going back to the 17th century which seeks to relate the sacrificial action of the Eucharist more directly to Christ's own sacrifice. Anglicans have expressed this in different ways. All are agreed that Christ's own sacrifice was offered "one for all," and many Anglicans would affirm that in some sense this sacrifice, without being repeated, is represented before God.

Modern New Testament exegesis offers a way to cut through all these dilemmas, inherited as they are largely from the Middle Ages. In most contemporary exegesis the words "body" and "blood" are interpreted increasingly not as substances but as saving event *(Heilsereignis)*. And with the biblical notion of *anamnesis* being brought into play, the once-for-all saving event can be understood as being rendered present in its saving efficacy. It was this scriptural-exegetical view of the words of institution and of the *anamnesis* command that undergirded the ARCIC statement on the Eucharist, known as the Windsor

17

statement. Following the precedent set by our common statement on justification, we have produced a common statement on Real Presence. The sacrificial aspect of the Eucharist still remains to be covered, particularly its relationship to the once-for-all sacrifice of Christ.

The Authority of Scripture

The last topic to be discussed and drawn together in a joint statement is the authority of scripture. Here the doctrinal situation in our respective communions and in relation to one another is not without its analogues to the situation in regard to the Holy Communion. There are streams in both communions (though not represented very much by the Episcopal branch of the Anglican Communion) which hold to a strong doctrine of scriptural inerrance and infallibility. Yet both communions have since the Enlightenment been through the traumas of biblical criticism. Later, both felt the impact of neo-orthodoxy and its subsequent demise in a renewed emphasis on the pluralism of the biblical witness and the time-conditioned character of its language and concept-uality (cf. Ernst Kasemann among Lutherans and Dennis Nineham among Anglicans). Exegetes, however, are beginning to see again that the one gospel is proclaimed in, with and through these pluralistic, time-conditioned human expressions. Most of us would see the authority of scripture as the Word of God or the gospel preached through the medium of human elements open to histori-cal criticism. Following the method of our statement of justification, the majority of us, it has transpired, are ready to move forward to a common affirmation of the authority of scripture as the Word of God in this sense. In this case, however, the differences are so great that a minority demural has been deemed necessary.

The Function of Joint Statements

Joint statements, such as LED II's statement on justification or the statements emanating from ARCIC, are not full confessions of faith. They deal with specific doctrinal *loci* which have been matters of differences between the communions in the dialogue. They do not say all that the participants (particularly one side) would want to say about the doctrinal *locus* in question. But they would include certain fundamental affirmations which should assure the participating communion which sets high store upon that doctrinal *locus,* that the other party, if it adopts the statement as representing its own faith, is in sufficient dogmatic agreement here to warrant continuing to work for ultimate ecclesial fellowship.

To some Anglicans the suggestion of dogmatic agreement on matters going beyond the Chicago-Lambeth Quadrilateral may seem strange. But the same Lambeth Conference which first promulgated the Quadrilateral as a pan-Anglican formula, placed it in the setting of a wider dogmatic system. And in one concordat of inter-communion which the Anglican Church has consummated in the present century, namely that with the Old Catholics, dogmatic agreement was stated by one of its principal architects on the Anglican side to be an essential prerequisite for such inter-communion. The dialogue is not, therefore, departing from Anglican tradition, but, stimulated by the dialogue with the Lutherans, Anglicans are returning to one of their fundamental principles.

To some Lutherans it may seem strange that limited agreement on controverted dogmatic *loci* should be thought adequate for some degree of ecclesial relationship, when the classical Lutheran position has been that the complete confessional agreement is essential for union. However, Dr. Rusch reports some change here in some recent Lutheran thinking. This is evident in two documents put out by the Lutheran World Federation entitled "More than Church Unity" and "Guidelines for Ecumenical Encounter." Here there is recognition for the first time of the possibility of multiple expressions of doctrine. A model of church unity for much of recent Lutheran theology is that of a fellowship in which confessional peculiarities are not blended but reconciled as legitimate pluralism. In such a pattern joint statements would represent an essential core of dogmatic agreement within a wider pluralism. The joint statement as a method of ecumenical dialogue might be graphically represented as follows:

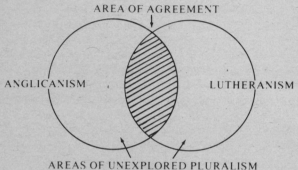

The shaded part of the diagram represents the doctrine covered by agreed statements, the rest of the circles those areas of doctrine covered by legitimate pluralism. The shaded area should, as in case of the doctrine of justification, assure the Lutherans that Episcopalians have a true understanding of what is to the Lutherans the essential core of the Gospel. At the same time, this should be a challenge to Anglicanism to recover the centrality of justification *propter Christum* in a way that has not been the case in its theology since the mid-nineteenth century, when it tended to be obscured by an idealistic and metaphysical theology of the incarnation.

Apostolic succession and the historic episcopate have played an analogous role in Anglicanism to the doctrine of justification in Lutheranism. As most Lutherans in the past could envisage pulpit and altar fellowship only on the basis of complete confessional agreement, so too Anglicans have usually thought of acceptance of the historic episcopate as a *sine qua non* of a minimal degree of intercommunion. Now recent Anglican thinking, in which LED I and the international Anglican-Lutheran dialogue have played a signal role, has shifted significantly. Behind the specific forms which the Anglican shape of polity (and it needs to be remembered that this is not solely Anglican: it is the shape which emerged in the early church and which is still maintained by Latin Catholicism and the Eastern Churches, Chalcedonian and non-Chalcedonian alike) lies something which is far more essential, ministry understood as a gift of the Lord to his church, and ordination as a "sacramental" act. If the Lutherans can accept an agreed statement on these lines, then we will have another juxtaposition of two circles with an overlapping area. Could Episcopalians agree that *in our present divided state,* and in a situation where a merger or organic reunion is not contemplated, the historic episcopate with its particular form of apostolic succession (not apostolic succession itself, which LED I agreed that Lutherans have preserved in a different form), belongs to the area of legitimate pluralism? For Anglicans, of course, acceptance of the historic episcopate remains a pre-condition for full communion and/or organic reunion.

The Place of Joint Statements in the Process of Dialogue

Stage 1 (completed)
> LED I. Discovery of wide areas of agreement and identification of areas of continuing difference for future discussion. Recommendations to church bodies: the areas of agreement constitute a sufficient basis for (1) mutual ecclesial recognition and (2)

limited eucharistic sharing; with the implementation of the first two recommendations as a precondition, (3) further dialogue (LED II) on areas of continuing difference.

Stage 2 (completed)

Reception of LED I report by church bodies. No action on recommendations (1) or (2) but initiation of LED II.

Stage 3 (completed)

LED II. Development of method: papers on controverted issues from each side; joint statements on justification, Eucharist, the nature of the Gospel, the authority of Scripture and Apostolicity; LED II Report containing joint statements, supporting papers from each side, and renewal of recommendations of LED I.

Stage 4 (for the future)

Reception by church bodies and implementation of recommendation.

Stage 5 (for the future)

LED III. Continuing dialogue on controverted areas not covered by joint statements of LED II.

Stage 6 (for the future)

Leading to the final goal of complete confessional agreement and full eucharistic sharing.

3.
Lutheran-Episcopal Dialogue II Joint Statements

Joint Statement on Justification

A. We the participants in the Lutheran-Episcopal Dialogue understand that our respective churches confess the gospel of Jesus Christ as God's saving word of grace to a fallen world. Together, we affirm that the gospel is the good news that for us and for our salvation God's Son was made man, fulfilled all righteousness, died and rose again from the dead according to the scriptures. Through the proclamation of this gospel in word and sacraments, the Holy Spirit calls, works faith, gathers, enlightens and sanctifies the whole Christian Church on earth and preserves it in union with Jesus Christ in the one true faith. The Spirit thereby leads us into a life of service and praise of God, the Father, the Son, and the Holy Spirit.

B. At the time of the Reformation, Anglicans and Lutherans shared a common confession and understanding of God's justifying grace, i.e. that we are accounted righteous before God only for the merit of our Lord and Savior Jesus Christ, by faith, and not for our own works or deservings. This good news of salvation continues to comfort the people of God and to establish them in the hope and promise of eternal life. In preaching and teaching, in liturgy and sacraments, both communions confess the radical gift of God's grace and righteousness in the crucified and risen Jesus Christ to the human race, which has no righteousness of its own.

C. In the western cultural setting in which our communions, Episcopal and Lutheran, find themselves, the gospel of justification continues to address the needs of human beings alienated from a holy and gracious God. Therefore, it is the task of the church to minister this gospel with vivid and fresh proclamation and to utilize all available resources for the theological enrichment of this ministry.

D. In both communions the understanding of the term "salvation" has had different emphases. Among Lutherans, salvation has commonly been synonymous with the forgiveness of sins; among Episcopalians, salvation has commonly included not only the forgiveness of sins but also the call to and promise of sanctification. As we continue to listen to each other, may God grant that

23

justification by grace and the new life in the Spirit abound.

E. We rejoice in these common convictions, and recommend them to our churches for reflection and use.

Joint Statement on the Gospel

God, who created and who continually sustains all that exists[1] out of that creation, brought forth humanity for eternal fellowship with himself.[2] Because such fellowship must be a relationship of freedom, humanity was originally given the free capacity to reject God's love. When human freedom was misused, as represented in Scripture by the story of the Fall,[3] this rebellion brought disorder to creation as a whole,[4] and in particular it brought disorder to human nature. God's love has sought constantly to reconcile humanity to himself[5] through the proclamation of the promise of salvation as he dealt with his people Israel. This divine activity has been effected by God's Holy Spirit,[6] and may be seen as the expression of grace. That grace has been fulfilled by God's entry into human life in the person of Jesus Christ.[7] He is the ultimate revelation of what God is like, whose actions and attitudes have shown what God intended human nature to be. As God made Man, Jesus Christ has been like us in all respects apart from sin,[8] but has identified himself with our sin and has claimed it for his own.[9] By taking that sin to the Cross, he has secured forgiveness for all sin. In raising Jesus Christ from death, God the Father has vindicated his sacrifice for our salvation. By grace, everyone who trusts entirely in God's mercy is set free from every burden of the past. In each life so redeemed God's Spirit operates through the gift of Christ who was uniquely annointed by the Holy Spirit for his saving work, for guidance, for perserverance and for the application of God's power in the world.[10] Thus fellowship with God and the divine image in humanity will be fully restored by a grace that can be received through *faith* that is not initiated by ourselves but is the gift of God.[11]

References

1 - Gen. 1:1
2 - Gen. 2:15
3 - Gen. 3:5
4 - Gen. 3:17
5 - John 3:16 & II Cor. 5:18
6 - The Nicene Creed - "Who has spoken through the prophets"
7 - Gal. 4:4
8 - Heb. 4:15
9 - II Cor. 5:21
10 - John 16:13-14 & Eph. 1:13-14
11 - Eph. 2:8-9

Joint Statement on Eucharistic Presence

1. In the period of the Reformation, the controversy over the Eucharist which affected Western Christendom as a whole was focused for Anglicans and Lutherans on the sacrifice of the Mass and Christ's presence in the sacrament. In the light of the recovery of the gospel of justification by faith, Lutherans rejected any notion of sacrifice which obscured the sufficiency and finality of Christ's sacrifice upon the cross and God's gracious gift of communion. Both traditions rejected a metaphysical explanation of the Real Presence (in particular the doctrine of transubstantiation), as well as interpretations of the Eucharist as a good work offered to God and meritorious for salvation. Both traditions affirmed a doctrine of the Lord's Supper conforming to the New Testament teaching in which Christ is both the gift and the giver. Lutherans defended the Real Presence of Christ's body and blood "in, with, and under" the forms of bread and wine in order to make the christological affirmation that God meets us in the humanity as well as the divinity of Christ in this means of grace. For them, this implied a two-fold eating of the sacrament, spiritually and orally (*Formula of Concord,* Solid Declaration

VII:60-61). Anglicans, on the other hand, followed the Reformed emphasis on the spiritual eating by faith, thus denying that the wicked and unbelievers partake of Christ (*Articles of Religion* 28-29). It was Richard Hooker (1554?-1600) who gave Anglicanism its normative approach to eucharistic doctrine by teaching that the elements of bread and wine are the instruments of participation in the body and blood of Christ. In more recent times, biblical studies and liturgical renewal have led Lutherans and Anglicans to recognize a convergence on the essentials of eucharistic faith and practice.

2. The eucharistic celebration of Word and Sacrament is the heart and center of the life and mission of the Church as the body of Christ in and for the world. It nourishes the community of the New Covenant, the family of God, whose corporate life is characterized by thanksgiving *(eucharistia).* Such corporate life serves in the world as a sign of the new creation initiated by God in Christ Jesus, so that through the Gospel the world may come to faith and that all people might be brought to unity with God and each other in Christ. The Eucharist enlivens the Church and strengthens our oneness in Christ. It is directly from the eucharistic table that we are sent forth into the world in the name of Christ, rejoicing in the power of his Spirit, strengthened and refreshed to do the work God has given us to do.

3. The presence of Christ in the Church is proclaimed in a variety of ways in the eucharistic liturgy. It is the risen Christ himself who presides at each assembly of his people: "where two or three are gathered together in my name, there am I in the midst of them." It is Christ who is promised and proclaimed in the readings of the Old and New Testaments. It is Christ who is represented by each of the baptized members and in a special way by the ordained ministers, as each fulfills a particular liturgical role, such diverse roles being complementary aspects of a

single liturgical action. It is Christ who gives himself in his body and blood as both our sacrifice and our feast.

Throughout Western Christianity, the Words of Institution *(Verba Christi)* have been generally seen as the focus of the consecration, although all would acknowledge that the presence of the Holy Spirit is essential to the Eucharist whether or not it is explicitly expressed. Eucharistic prayer encompasses proclamation, remembrance, and supplication.[1] Within the framework of this thanksgiving, the Church proclaims its faith through the memorial of Christ in the events of salvation history and the supplication of the Holy Spirit to build up the unity of God's people through faithful reception of the body and blood of Christ.

4. The Church's celebration of the Eucharist rests upon the Word and authority of Christ, who commanded his disciples to remember him in this way until his return. According to his word of promise, Christ's very body broken on the cross and his very blood shed for the forgiveness of our sins are present, distributed and received, as a means of partaking here and now of the fruits of that atoning sacrifice. This is also the presence of the risen and glorified Christ who pleads for us before the throne of God. It is not our faith that effects this presence of our Lord, but by the faith we have received, the blessings of the Lord's suffering, death, and resurrection are sealed to us until he comes again in glory.

5. The Lord who comes to his people in the power of the Holy Spirit and by means of his Word "in, with, and under" the forms of bread and wine enables all Christians to avail themselves of the benefits of his saving death and life-giving resurrection. By partaking of the sacrament, the community of faith created by Baptism is manifested as the Body of Christ in and for the world, and empowered to live a godly life. We may speak of a sacramental transformation of the called and gathered

people of God into the image of Christ, that we may be, in Luther's words, "Christ to our neighbor."

For this reason the Church has desired a steady access to the Word of God and the Sacrament of the Altar. In both of our Churches, more of our parishes are scheduling weekly celebrations of the Eucharist as the main Sunday and festival Service. As the frequency of celebration increases for the whole congregation, there is a desire to include the sick and the homebound in the congregation's Eucharist. This is an ancient practice, and as an extension of the distribution of the sacrament it accords with the true use of the institution.* Both Lutherans and Episcopalians would want to disavow a veneration of the reserved elements that is dissociated from the eucharistic celebration of the congregation.[2]

The true use of the sacrament is to eat and drink the body and blood in the faith that our Lord's words give what they promise. Luther's *Small Catechism* asserts that "By these words the forgiveness of sins, life, and salvation are given to us in the sacrament, for where there is forgiveness of sins, there are also life and salvation." (Tappert, p. 352). The Catechism in the *Book of Common Prayer* amplifies the same benefits of the sacrament: "The benefits we receive are the forgiveness of our sins, the strengthening of our union with Christ and one another, and the foretaste of the heavenly banquet which is our nourishment in eternal life" (BCP, pp. 859-860).

6. In recent years, through biblical scholarship, there has been a growing appreciation of the eschatological dimension of the Lord's Supper. The Lord who comes to his people by the power of his Word and Spirit is the risen and glorified Lord. In Holy Baptism we are joined to the death and resurrection of Christ and made members of his body to be living signs of the new creation in Christ. In the eucharistic celebration we not only receive the

*FC, Solid Declaration, VII, *passim.*

strength to become what we are called to be, but also participate in the joys of the age to come when Christ will be all in all. The Eucharist manifests the unity of the Church in Christ here and now, and anticipates the oneness of all creation under the reign of Christ. For this reason, communion among separated Christians is to be sought wherever sufficient agreement on Word and Sacraments can be reached.[3]

FOOTNOTES

1. Eucharistic prayer encompasses the liturgical material between the *Sursum corda* and the distribution. The elements of proclamation, remembrance, and supplication are found in classical Lutheran communion rites, such as those in *The Common Service* (1888) and *The Lutheran Hymnal* (1941), in the eucharistic prefaces with their praise of God for redemption in Christ, the Lord's Prayer with its supplicatory petitions, and the Words of Institution, which are both proclamation and remembrance ("in the night in which He was betrayed, our Lord Jesus Christ took bread . . .").

2. Differences arise between those who would practice reservation for (communion) only, and those who would also regard it as a means of eucharistic devotion. For the latter, adoration of Christ in the reserved sacrament should be regarded as an extension of eucharistic worship, even though it does not include immediate sacramental reception, which remains the primary purpose of reservation. Any dissociation of such devotion from this primary purpose, which is communion in Christ of all his members, is a distortion in eucharistic practice." ('The Elucidations' of the Windsor Statement on Eucharistic Doctrine, par. 8; *Agreed Statements*, Cincinnati, Ohio: Forward Movement Publications, 1980, pp. 32-33. Cf. Lutheran/Roman Catholic Joint Commission: *The Eucharist;* Geneva: The Lutheran World Federation, 1980, par. 53, p. 19; and also *The Book of Common Prayer* (1979), pp. 408-409).

3. The concluding sentence does not imply that all Lutherans and Episcopalians believe that such "sufficient agreement" has been achieved. Areas for further examination in future dialogues would laudably include:
   1) the theology of the consecration and its practical consequences in regard to the elements;
   2) the pastoral concern in administration (open and closed Communion);
   3) further clarification of the doctrine of the Real Presence;
   4) the concept of 'sacrifice' in the Eucharist;
   5) the relation of the Eucharist to the historic episcopate.

Joint Statement
On The Authority of Scripture

We agree that the Holy Scripture of the Old and New Testament is the "rule and ultimate standard of faith" (Lambeth Conference of 1888, Resolution 11 a; cf. *Formula of Concord,* Epitome 1: 'the only rule and norm" (Tappert 464). Holy Scripture is the ultimate standard by which all of tradition, whether creeds, confessions, or Councils, is to be judged. Those who wrote Scripture were inspired by the Holy Spirit to put down the pure testimony of what God has said and done, and as the heart and center of Scripture, what he has said and done in our Savior Jesus Christ. Through the Holy Spirit the Church continues to hear the Holy Scripture as God speaking to his people. As a consequence, the Church has used Scripture as its normative guide for faith and life. Therefore the Church is able to proclaim the Word of God with authority and evaluate life with prophetic power.

Holy Scripture needs to be expounded because language changes and because the Church faces problems which did not exist in Biblical times. But expositions vary, and sin corrupts; the pure testimony to Jesus Christ, our only Savior, is then endangered. The Holy Spirit, through means such as creeds, confessions, and Councils, has provided guides for correctly expounding Holy Scripture. These are secondary guides, subject to the ultimate standard of Holy Scriputre, and they, like Holy Scripture, are also in need of exposition because language changes and new problems arise. Here, too, God through the power of his Word and Spirit continues to lead and guide his Church as he directs the Church's attention to Jesus Christ as found in Holy Scriputre.

All members of the Church share in expounding what Holy Scripture means for their faith and life, using all their gracious God has given them, including reason, to carry out this task. In addition, certain individuals have been given special gifts by the Spirit for discerning what Holy Scripture means for their place and time. Because of their authority or training, such individuals are able to be especially helpful in expounding Scripture for their time. On account of the vagaries of history and the corruption of sin, all members of the Church, even those with special gifts, remain subject for both faith and life to their Lord Jesus Christ as found in the ultimate standard of Holy Scripture.

In both communions there are varieties of understanding and application of Scripture. These differences and tensions are not without weight; however, they are not differences between Lutherans and Episcopalians. These are problems which we have in common and we might more helpfully face them together.

Dissenting Statement Attached

Although there are excellent points in the paper on "Authority of Scripture," as a matter of conscience we herewith dissent from its adoption owning to perceived areas of ambiguity therein which we deem would cause confusion and be detrimental to the best interests of the Lutheran Church-Missouri Synod.

The Rev. Carl L. Bornman

The Rev. Jerald C. Joersz

Joint Statement on Apostolicity

Introduction

During our discussions the Lutheran and Episcopalian participants have been happily surprised by the substantial agreement which we share with regard to the Church's apostolicity. The following statement indicates the lines of this convergence while pointing out areas of divergence where appropriate.

Part One: Apostolicity: A New Appreciation

(1) The Apostolicity of the Church refers to the Church's continuity with Christ and the apostles in its movement through history. The Church is apostolic as "devoted . . . to the apostles' teaching and fellowship, to the breaking of bread and the prayers." (Acts 2:42)

(2) Apostolicity or apostolic succession is a dynamic, diverse reality organically embracing a variety of elements and activities. It includes continued faithfulness to the apostles' teaching, which teaching found normative expression in Holy Scripture, and under Scripture, in the ecumenical creeds. It involves participation in baptism, in the apostles' prayers and the breaking of bread which continues in the liturgical and sacramental life of the Church. Abiding in apostolic fellowship is given expression through sharing in the Church's common life of mutual edification and caring, served by an ecclesiastically called and recognized pastoral ministry of Word and sacrament. Finally, apostolic succession involves a continuing involvement in the apostolic mission, in being sent into the world to share the Gospel of Christ by proclamation to all far and near and by neighborly service to those in need.

(3) It has been all too common for many to think of apostolic succession primarily in terms of historic episcopate. We must take care to avoid this narrowing of our view of the Church's apostolic succession to an exclusive concern with the historic episcopate. Such a reduction falsely isolates the historic episcopate and also obscures the fact that churches may exhibit most aspects of apostolicity while being weak or deficient in some. Recovery of appreciation for the wider dimensions of apostolicity has allowed us to see in each other a commonality which a narrow concentration on the historic episcopate would have obscured.

Part Two: The Historical Development of Lutheran and Episcopalian Views and Expressions of Apostolic Succession

Different aspects of apostolicity have appeared throughout the Church's history and continue to shape the Church's faith, life and mission today. We note the following developments.

Three forms of apostolicity emerge in the early Church especially directed toward the threat of the Gnostics in the areas of (1) doctrine, (2) worship and (3) order. (1) The canon of prophetic and apostolic Scripture is set as the recognized authoritative norm or rule of doctrine. Apostolic "rules of faith" in creedal form develop, not only to guard against heresy and to instruct catechumens, but also (2) for use in baptismal liturgies as interrogatory creeds or as summaries of the faith for the newly baptized. Concomitant with this was the development of influential liturgies which helped protect apostolic authenticity in the celebration of Word and sacrament. (3) Apostolic succession was wedded to succession of bishops in sees so that bishops were looked to as guardians of apostolic faith and practice, representing the teaching authority of the apostles.

In the middle ages, mission became again clearly linked to apostolic succession, as in the missionary journeys of St. Paul. Missionary bishops were sent to spread Christianity throughout Europe; in other cases, missionaries like Boniface were subsequently made bishops.

The developments which led to a break between East and West in 1054 helped focus juridical authority in Rome, making the "Apostolic See" more and more the authoritative arbiter of theology and giving the Roman rite an increasingly normative character.

Both Lutheran and Anglican reformers rejected the Papacy as the primary focus of continuity in the Gospel.

Lutherans saw faithfulness to the apostles' teaching in Scripture as the core of apostolicity. In England a similar recovery of biblical faith had been brewing. The Anglican reform began with polity when the problems of royal succession occasioned the break with Rome. Liturgical and doctrinal reform, which had been in ferment even before the break with Rome, followed. However, the metro-political government and diocesan structure remained intact in the Church of England. From this emerged the characteristic Anglican appeal to the bishops as signs and guardians of apostolicity in liturgy and doctrine. The German *Landeskirchen* and Scandinavian folk-churches were conditioned by princely prerogative (viz. *cuius regio, eius religio*). Sweden and Finland retained historic episcopal succession. For Lutheranism as a whole, the episcopate in apostolic succession did not function as the primary strand of apostolicity. The confessional writings, the Augsburg Confession and the Small Catechism in Scandinavia and the entire Book of Concord in Germany, served to focus the Lutheran understanding of apostolicity on *doctrinal continuity*. While the Anglicans had their 39 Articles (which showed significant Lutheran and some Reformed influence), the Book of Common Prayer tended to include liturgy as central to apostolic continuity.

In matters of reforming the doctrine, liturgy and polity of the Church, both communions showed high regard for tradition and resisted that version of *sola scriptura* which held that only what Scripture commands is to be retained. Rather, they kept whatever Scripture did not forbid if it had proved beneficial to the Church and consistent with the Gospel.

Cranmer, Hooker, and the Caroline divines of the 17th century were careful not to "un-Church" those continental Protestants who did not maintain the historic episcopate. Ironically it was the challenge of some of the Puritans

34

who contended that episcopal government was not biblical which tended to harden certain Anglican defenses of Episcopacy in apostolic succession.[1] It was not until the Anglo-Catholicism of the 19th century Tractarian movement that serious argument was heard within the Church of England for the historic episcopate being of the essence (*esse*) of the Church in a way that tended to "un-Church" non-episcopal churches. In recent decades, most Episcopalians have argued either for the episcopacy as an order of ministry developed under the Spirit's guidance for the well-being (*bene esse*) of the Church or as an aspect of the fullness of the Church (*plene esse*)[2]— both groups holding it to be a sign, symbol and means of the Church's unity and continuty in mission and ministry, doctrine and worship.

The Lutheran reformers, while supportive of the office of bishop, were critical of abuses of episcopal power. Bishops have no power apart from the Word of God to make new laws, institute new rites or create traditions, as though one would sin by omitting them or could be justified by doing them (CA, XXVIII, p. 56; Apology, Art XV, p. 31; and XXVIII, pp. 8-14). Bishops ought not impose heavy burdens on people, taking no account of human weakness (CA XXIII, p. 16; Apology, Art. IV, p. 233). On the contrary, "the power of bishops is a power or command of God to preach the Gospel, to remit or retain sins, and to administer sacraments." (CA, XXVIII, p. 5).

Lutheran Church life after the Reformation was focused around the ministry of Word and sacraments administered by those ecclesiastically called to the pastoral office. In the 19th century controversies arose in Europe and America over the doctrine of the ministry which have carried over into the 20th century. These controversies involved emphasizing *either* the functions of the pastor of proclaiming the Word and administering the Sacraments *or* the pastor's personal representation of Christ.[3] Another dimension of the controversy centers on ordination, understood *on the one hand* as delegation or even transference from the royal priesthood in a local congregation and *on the other hand* as recognition by the larger Church (e.g., the Synod) of an office bestowed by the Lord through ordained clergy on persons ecclesiastically called.[4] All groups agreed that the call came ultimately from God.

During the modern era, all Scandinavian Lutherans retained the office and title of bishop. In the 20th century many German "general superintendents" were given the title *bishop* and three American churches have adopted the title since 1970 for their synod or district presidents. In Baltic and Slavic countries the title *bishop* is used. Some Lutheran churches in Africa have bishops and the Lutheran Church in Papua New Guinea has recently adopted the term.

Part Three: An Analysis of the Agreement in Apostolic Succession to be Found in the Lutheran and Episcopal Churches

It is important to state plainly the high degree of commonality which is to be found between the Lutheran and Episcopal Churches in the various aspects of the Church's apostolicity. We will look briefly at each of the main aspects, keeping in mind that these aspects interrelate and are treated separately only for purposes of analysis.

(1) Apostolic Mission

Preoccupation with things at home at the time of the Reformation delayed a vital engagement in overseas missions on the part of both Anglicans and Lutherans. Subsequently both Lutherans and Anglicans have been extensively involved in missionary outreach. At the beginning of the modern missionary era there was a significant convergence of Anglican and Lutheran efforts. The first Protestant missionaries sent to India (German Lutherans named Plütschau and Ziegenbalg) were commissioned by the King of Denmark; later they came under the auspices of the S.P.C.K. The call of our Lord to "go into all the world" is clearly recognized by both churches. Actual participation has varied in both.

In an increasingly secular culture both communions must also recognize a new urgency in the call to evangelize those who live nearer to home. Social concern and acts of neighborliness are espoused by both Lutherans and Episcopalians in the name of Christ. The Lutheran doctrine of the "two kingdoms" (God's two-fold rule in all areas, secular and spiritual) has not always realized its social potential. The Episcopalian understanding of the church's social responsibility has in some places given way to the "suburban captivity of the churches." Both churches have experienced, in Europe and America, the negative Erastian effects of Caesaropapism—especially in times of war. Both Lutherans and Episcopalians have had glorious moments and sad declines in this aspect of apostolic succession.

(2) Apostolic Scriptures

The Lutheran churches and the Episcopal church acknowledge the writings of the Old and New Testaments to be the normative means of abiding in continuity with apostolic teaching. In this the two Communions are at one with each other and with the early Church which first recognized the canonical status of the inspired writings. By adhering to the same canonical writings, by assigning portions of them to be read in corporate worship, by sharing in large measure the same lectionary, by interpreting these writings in teaching and preaching, and by appealing to these writings as the Apostles' test of true doctrine and life, Lutherans and Episcopalians are at one.

(3) Apostolic Creeds

Following a precedent already established in the days of the apostles, the church by the second century had formulated creeds. These creeds or "rules of faith," which were customarily trinitarian in structure, summarized the apostles' teaching and served as a guide and guard for the faith of the Church against errors such as Gnosticism. The use and the development of these rules of faith as doctrinal summaries and as interrogatory creeds in the baptismal rite was influenced by the catechumenate.

Due to the struggle with heresy and the attempt of the Church to interpret faith in the context of Hellenistic culture, the creeds of the ecumenical councils — unlike the earlier creedal formulations — used terminology not explicitly found in Scripture. Reflecting the Christological definitions of the Councils of Ephesus and Chalcedon, the Athanasian Creed (BCP, p. 864; LBW, pp. 54-55) of the 5th or 6th century described the mystery of Christ's person and expanded Nicene trinitarian theology.

Historically, both the Lutheran and Anglican communions have treasured and affirmed these creeds and confessed them in their worship, teaching, and preaching.

(4) The Holy Sacraments

It is from the written apostolic testimony that we receive our Lord's commands to forgive sins, to commune, and to baptize. Lutherans and Episcopalians agree that Baptism and the Lord's Supper, ordained by Christ, are necessary to Christian life and worship.[5] Furthermore, the importance that absolution and ordination have had for both communions cannot be minimized historically, theologically, or liturgically. Remarkable similarities exist in the Lutheran and Episcopalian liturgies of Baptism, Holy Communion, Confession and Forgiveness, Ordination, and Morning and Evening Prayer. This is seen not only in the worship forms emerging from the liturgical movements of the 19th and 20th centuries (which demonstrate significant Anglican influence upon Lutheran rites) but also in the 16th Century which saw Lutheran influences on the Book of Common Prayer.[6]

(5) The Ordained Ministry or Pastoral Office

(a) This is a most controversial area in the discussions between Lutherans and Episcopalians regarding apostolicity. It is therefore important to note that even here we have a great measure of agreement not always found with other communions. The common aspects are:

(i) Both Lutherans and Episcopalians hold the ordained ministry of Word and Sacrament to be of divine instituion. They distinguish this pastoral office from the priesthood of all believers, while holding at the same time that it is one of the primary tasks of the ordained ministry to equip the saints for their work of ministry (priesthood of all believers). (CA V; Articles of Religion XXIII).

(ii) The two communions both engage in the practice of ordination. Entrance into the pastoral office or holy orders is bestowed through a liturgical act which is not to be repeated.[7] Ordination is presided over by those set apart in the Church so to ordain in the Name of God. The language of sacrament is not always used of ordination in either Communion, but the ritual aspects of a sacramental act are always present in both (i.e., the Word of God, prayer and the laying-on-of-hands).

(iii) Both Lutherans and Episcopalians intend by ordination to set apart ministers of both Word and Sacrament.

(iv) Both hold that the succession in office of ordained ministers shows the Church's continuity in time and space in the ministry of Word and Sacrament and the care of the Church.

(v) Both Lutherans and Episcopalians recognize the necessity of oversight *(episcopē)* which is embodied in an ordained office. Lutherans see *episcopē* exercised in the ministry of parish pastors as well as in bishops' supervision of local congregations and clergy, while Episcopalians see that *episcopē* as shared by bishops with their clergy.

(vi) Episcopalians recognize that Lutherans do affirm the full dignity of the pastoral office and are open to the historic episcopate as a valid and proper form of that office. Some Lutheran Churches are ordered in the historic episcopate. There is even a preference for the historic episcopate shown in the Lutheran confessional writings where and when that form could be maintained in accord with the Gospel, i.e., in the context of faithful preaching of the Word and the right administration of the Sacraments. Lutherans do not, however, hold the historic episcopate to be the only legitimate form of *episcopē*.

(b) Since both Lutherans and Episcopalians are in official bi-lateral discussions with Roman Catholics, we in this discussion take great encouragement from two findings of the Lutheran-Roman Catholic discussions which give strong support to the positions which we have developed in our report.

First we note that the Roman Catholic-Lutheran discussions in the U.S.A. indicate large areas of agreement in the Faith. They further noted the diversity of church order found in the New Testament period. In the light of the practice of presbyteral succession found within the succession of the Roman Church, the Roman Catholic partners in the discussion recommend that Rome recognize the validity of Lutheran Orders as presently constituted.[8] (See Appendix #1 for excerpts.)

Next we note that in Roman Catholic theology,

reflected in the international discussions between Lutheran and Roman Catholic Churches, a distinction is made between Apostolic Succession in substance (the apostolic succession of the whole Church in faith and life) and apostolic succession of ministerial transmission (the succession of ministers) which is the sign and servant of the Apostolic Succession of the whole Church. This distinction is essentially the same as we have made. It allows the Roman Catholic partners to raise the question whether it is possible to affirm Lutheran orders to be within the true succession of the Church and therefore merely defective in form or lacking fullness and not invalid. (See appendix #2, Malta N. 57, 58, and 63 and forthcoming statement on "The Ministry in the Church" of the international dialogue.)

Surely if Roman Catholics and Lutherans are coming to such an awareness of existing agreement in the area of the ordained ministry it behooves Episcopalians and Lutherans to see if such agreement does not also exist among us. We in this discussion have concluded that it does exist.

Conclusion

There is, it is to be admitted, serious divergence in the actual ordering of the Pastoral Office in the two Communions as well as in the importance generally accorded to the historic episcopate. Further, there are additional topics worthy of continued discussion.[9] However, despite that, we are profoundly impressed and encouraged by the basic and extensive elements of agreement which we have found in all of the aspects of apostolic succession, including that of the ordained ministry. We can declare together that both the Lutheran Church and the Episcopal Church stand in Apostolic Succession. "And they devoted themselves to the apostles' teaching and fellowship, to the breaking of bread and prayers." (Acts 2:42)

FOOTNOTES

1. At the Restoration of the English Monarchy and the Church of England as episcopally ordered (1660-62), a new phrase was added at the conclusion of the following statement from the Preface to the Ordinal in the 1662 Book of Common Prayer:

   And therefore, to the intent that these Orders may be continued, and reverently used and esteemed in this Church, no man shall be accounted or taken to be a lawful Bishop, Priest, or Deacon, in this Church, or suffered to execute any of the said Functions, except he be called, tried, examined, and admitted thereunto, according to the Form hereafter following, *or hath had Episcopal Consecration or Ordination*.

   Emphatically, this was not an attempt to un-Church continental Protestants, but rather to deal directly with a controverted point of polity within the English Church (in and after 1662 those clergy who could or would not accept this stipulation — Nonconformists — where legally ejected or barred from clerical office/livings within the Church of England as by law established). Certain difficulties within the Church of England that continued to touch upon this point of polity, e.g., the Bangorian Controversy (1717-19) and the Methodist Movement later in the century, resulted for some Highchurchmen in an increasingly rigorous interpretation of the necessity of episcopacy to authentic ecclesial life. But, again, this was understood *not* to un-Church continental Protestants.

2. It should be noted that the Consultation on Church Union (COCU), of which the Episcopal Church is a constituent member, has accepted the historic episcopate in its proposed order for a Church of Christ Uniting while not articulating any particular theory with regard to the terms mentioned in this paragraph. With respect to differing interpretations within contemporary Anglicanism, cf. Kenneth Kirk (ed.), *The Apostolic Ministry* (1946) — *esse* position; Stephen Neill (ed.), *The Ministry of the Church* (1947) — *bene esse* position; Kenneth Carey (ed.), *The Historic Episcopate in the Fullness of the Church* (1954) — *plene esse* position.

3. Holsten Fagerberg, *A New Look at the Lutheran Confessions.* (St. Louis, Concordia, 1972), pp. 226-238.

4. Theodore G. Tappert (ed.), *Lutheran Confessional Theology in America, 1840-1880.* (New York: Oxford University Press, 1972), pp. 229-245, 279.

5. The XXXIX Articles, Articles XXV, and the Catechism of the Book of Common Prayer, p. 854, called these "the sacraments of the gospel." The usage of later Lutheranism limited the sacraments to two in number, but in the Apology of the Augsburg Confession

(Book of Concord, Tappert edition, pp. 187.41, 211.4, 212.11-13; cf. pp. 310-313), Melanchthon includes Absolution among the sacraments and even allows that Ordination may be so designated. Melanchthon is operating here with a definition of sacraments in terms of Word-plus-*rite*. Luther tended to operate with a Word-plus-*element* definition, hence usually designated only two sacraments. (Cf. the Book of Common Prayer on other sacramental rites, p. 860).

6. It is noted that the Lutheran law-gospel dialectic may have influenced the adoption of the reading of the Law in the 1552 BCP. Martin Bucer's influence here is clear, but the possible Lutheran theological roots of this practice (even though it did not take hold in Lutheran liturgical practice) hold out some fascinating comparisons between Anglicanism and Lutheranism.

7. This non-repeatability refers to orders recognized within the two communions and does not deal with the issue of a mutually recognized ministry as between Lutherans and Episcopalians.

8. *Eucharist and Ministry: Lutherans and Catholics in Dialogue* (Minneapolis; Augsburg Publishing House, 1979), especially pp. 7-22.

9. The following weighty matters we believe require further discussion: 1) the relationship between presbyteral succession and episcopal succession, including a discussion of the role and office of the bishop; 2) the relation of the pastoral office to the priesthood-of-all-believers; 3) the possibility of a mutually recognized ministry of Word and Sacrament; and 4) the question of the ordination of women.

Several other matters are worthy of consideration and reflect issues which exist within both communions: 1) the exegetical basis of the institution of the ordained ministry; 2) the place of the charismatic ministry as found in the New Testament; and 3) the Papacy.

Appendix I

Material from *Lutherans and Catholics in Dialogue*, Volume IV, entitled *Eucharist and Ministry*

The Structuring of the Special Ministry.

19. Although we agree that Christ has given his church a special order of Ministry, we must also acknowledge the diverse ways in which this Ministry has been structured and implemented in the Catholic and Lutheran traditions.

20. In Catholicism, the Ministry of order has been apportioned among three Ministries or major orders: deacon, priest *(presbyter)*, and bishop. . . . Without prejudice to their belief that it is the bishop who possesses the fullness of the Ministry conferred by ordination Catholics note that it is both historically and theologically significant that priests have ordained others as priests.*

*Footnote 16 p. 14 DS 1145-1146, 1290, Cf. Fransen, "Orders and Ordination," in *Sacramentum Mundi,* vol. 4, esp. p. 316; Kilian McDonnell, "Ways of Validating Ministry," *Journal of Ecumenical Studies 7* (1970), 209-265; Arthur Carl Piepkorn, "The Sacred Ministry and Holy Ordination in the Symbolical Books of the Lutheran Church," pp. 116-117.

No subsequent footnotes are reproduced in this appendix. See original publication, Chapter Three, "Reflections of the Roman Catholic Participants," pp. 23-33.

* * *

Reflections of the Roman Catholic Participants

Introduction

36. At first glance the Roman Catholic attitude toward the Lutheran eucharistic Ministry would seem easily determinable. A simplified expression of the traditional Roman Catholic outlook is that those who preside at the eucharist do so in virtue of being ordained by a bishop who stands in succession to the apostles. . . . Thus the Lutheran eucharistic Ministry would seem to be deficient in what Catholics have hitherto regarded as essential elements.

37. Yet, as we Catholics in this dialogue have examined the problem, our traditional objections to the Lutheran

eucharistic Ministry were seen to be of less force today, and reasons emerged for a positive reappraisal. We may group our reflections below under the headings of historical arguments and theological arguments.

Historical Arguments

38. It is impossible to prove from the New Testament that the only Ministers of the eucharist were the apostles, their appointed successors, and those ordained by their successors. Modern biblical investigations have shown that there were several different concepts of "apostle" in the New Testament. . . .

39. At the beginning of the second century (but perhaps even earlier), as attested by Ignatius of Antioch, the bishop had emerged as the highest authority in the local church, and either he or his appointee presided at the eucharist. However, we are not certain how the Ignatian bishop was appointed or that he stood in a chain of historic succession to the apostles by means of ordination or even that the pattern described by Ignatius was universal in the church. Some find in Didache 10:7 evidence that wandering charismatic prophets could preside at the eucharist.

40. When the episcopate and the presbyterate had become a general pattern in the church, the historical picture still presents uncertainties that affect judgment on the Minister of the eucharist. For instance, is the difference between a bishop and a priest of divine ordination? St. Jerome maintained that it was not, and the Council of Trent, wishing to respect Jerome's opinion, did not undertake to define that the preeminence of the bishop over presbyters was a divine law. If the difference is not of divine ordination, the reservation to the bishop of the power of ordaining Ministers of the eucharist would be a church decision. In fact, in the history of the church there are instances of priests (i.e. presbyters)

ordaining other priests, and there is evidence that the church accepted and recognized the Ministry of priests so ordained.

41. By way of summation, we find from the historical evidence that by the sixteenth century there had been a long and almost exclusive practice whereby the only Minister of the eucharist was one ordained by a bishop who had been consecrated as heir to a chain of episcopal predecessors. Yet, in this long history there are lacunae, along with exceptions that offer some precedent for the practice adopted by the Lutherans.

Theological Arguments

42. The negative appraisal of the Lutheran eucharistic Ministry that has been traditional among Catholics was not based solely or even chiefly on an analysis of the historical evidence favoring episcopal ordination. Theological factors entered prominently into this appraisal. Here again, however, as we Catholic participants in the dialogue examined the difficulties, we found that they no longer seemed insuperable.

43. A. The question of an authentic eucharistic Ministry in a worshipping community is intimately related to an evaluation of that community as part of the church. . . . We are now obliged to reassess whether the Lutheran communities may not be churches that truly celebrate the holy eucharist.

44. B. It may be objected that while the Lutheran communities do constitute churches, they are defective churches in an essential note that has ramifications for the eucharistic Ministry, namely, apostolicity. This charge is true if apostolicity is defined so as necessarily to include apostolic succession through episcopal consecration. However, it is dubious that apostolicity should be so defined. In the first two centuries of Christianity apostolic succession in doctrine (fidelity to the gospel) was

considered more important than simple succession in office or orders. The lists of bishops that appeared late in the second century were intended to demonstrate more a line of legitimatized teachers than a line of sacramental validity. Undoubtedly apostolic succession through episcopal consecration is a valuable sign and aspect of apostolicity, for in church history there is a mutual interplay between doctrinal integrity and the succession of those who are its official teachers. Yet, despite the lack of episcopal succession, the Lutheran church by its devotion to gospel, creed, and sacrament has preserved a form of doctrinal apostolicity.

45. C. In the past, Catholics commonly assumed that Lutherans did not believe in the real presence of Christ's body and blood, sacramentally offered in the eucharistic sacrifice, and consequently were presumably not ordaining a eucharistic Ministry . . . we Catholics and Lutherans affirmed our agreement on the real presence and on the sacrificial character of the Lord's supper.

46. D. Still another Catholic difficulty about the Lutheran eucharistic Ministry arose from a fear that the Lutheran understanding of the sacred Ministry was defective. In examining a number of points discussed below, we found that, while there are differences of emphasis and phrasing in the theologies of our respective churches, there is also a gratifying degree of agreement as to the essentials of the sacred Ministry.

47. 1) Do Lutherans recognize that the sacred Ministry is of divine institution? We find the Lutheran affirmation: "God instituted the sacred Ministry of teaching the gospel and administering the sacraments."

48. 2) Do Lutherans conceive of the sacred Ministry as simply or primarily a Ministry of the word (preaching) rather than of sacrament? We have found a frequent joining of word and sacrament in the Lutheran writings on the subject. It is true that in the sixteenth century the

Lutherans gave emphasis to a Ministry of the word in reaction to what they saw as a danger of a purely ritualistic Ministry. In response, Catholics tended to give emphasis to the dispensation of the sacraments lest the importance of that factor in Ministry of denigrated. In the less apologetic atmosphere currently prevailing, both groups see that the task of the Ministry includes both word and sacrament.

49. 3) Do Lutherans see the sacred Ministry as something beyond or distinct from the general ministry of all believers? It is quite clear that the Lutherans have a concept of a special Ministry in the church. . . . Theologians of both churches need to clarify further the relation between clergy and laity and to analyze the biblical concept of the royal priesthood of God's people in order to see if that concept really tells us anything about eucharistic Ministry.

50. 4) Do Lutherans recognize the sacramentality of ordination to the sacred Ministry? Actually on one occasion in the Lutheran confessional documents, the term "sacrament" is deemed applicable to ordination, but such language is not common in Lutheran theology . . . We heard the affirmation that "The church has the command to appoint Ministers . . . God approves the Ministry and is present in it." "All three American Lutheran churches understand the Ministry of clergymen to be rooted in the Gospel." "Like the Roman Catholic, the Lutheran too sees ordination as conferring a spiritual authority on the recipient in a once-for-all fashion — namely; the power to sanctify through proclamation . . . of the word of God and the administration of the sacraments."

51. E. Perhaps the most serious obstacle standing in the way of a favorable Catholic evaluation of the Lutheran eucharistic Ministry has been the doctrine of the Council of Trent pertinent to sacred orders. In particular, canon

10 of Session VII (A.D. 1547; DS 1610) denied that all Christians have the power of administering all the sacraments, and canon 7 of Session XXIII (A.D. 1563; DS 1777) said that those who had not been ordained or commissioned by ecclesiastical or canonical power were not legitimate Ministers of the word and the sacraments. It would seem, *prima facie,* that in Trent's judgment Lutheran Ministers, since they have not been ordained by bishops, would not have the power of presiding at the eucharist, and that the Catholic church could not change its stance on this question since the doctrine of Trent is permanently binding. Yet cautions are in order. The Council of Trent was not concerned primarily with passing judgment on the sacred orders of the Reformed communities but with defending the legitimacy of the Catholic priesthood against Protestant attacks. The Tridentine assessment of Protestant ideas about the Ministry is detected chiefly through the implications of its condemnations of anti-Catholic theories. In the anathemas formulated against "Those who say . . ." there is no indication of whether Lutherans are meant in distinction from Calvinists, Zwinglians, Anabaptists, etc. Because of these difficulties, it is not easy to determine Trent's attitude toward the Lutheran eucharistic Ministry and the permanent value of that attitude.

52. One approach to the problem is the contention that the Tridentine attitude was not so absolutely negative as has been thought. Some are not sure that the council meant that a Minister "not ordained by ecclesiastical or canonical power" was really incapable of celebrating the eucharist. They emphasize that all that the council said was that this was not a "lawful" Ministry . . . .

53. Another approach to the Tridentine position reckons with the likelihood that the council really did mean implicitly to declare invalid Lutheran orders in the sixteenth century but wonders whether the present

situation is not so changed that the Tridentine attitude is now only partially applicable . . . without settling the question of the past, one might well conclude that the abuses Trent rejected are not present now.

54. The historical and theological reflections made above move us to doubt whether Roman Catholics should continue to question the eucharistic presence of the Lord in the midst of the Lutherans when they meet to celebrate the Lord's supper. And so we make the following statement:

As Roman Catholic theologians, we acknowledge in the spirit of Vatican II that the Lutheran communities with which we have been in dialogue are truly Christian churches, possessing the elements of holiness and truth that mark them as organs of grace and salvation. Furthermore, in our study we have found serious defects in the arguments customarily used against the validity of the eucharistic Ministry of the Lutheran churches. In fact, we see no persuasive reason to deny the possibility of the Roman Catholic church recognizing the validity of this Ministry. Accordingly we ask the authorities of the Roman Catholic church whether the ecumenical urgency flowing from Christ's will for unity may not dictate that the Roman Catholic church recognize the validity of the Lutheran Ministry, and correspondingly, the presence of the body and blood of Christ in the eucharistic celebrations of the Lutheran churches.

55. Lest we be misunderstood, we wish to add the following clarifications:

a. While this statement has implications for the question of Lutheran orders in the past, we have not made that question the focus of our discussions, and we do not think it necessary to solve that problem in order to make the present statement. Nor do we attempt to decide whether recognition by the Roman Catholic church would be constitutive of validity or merely confirmatory of existing validity.

56. b. By appealing for church action we stress our belief that the problem should be resolved by the respective churches and not on the level of private action by Ministers and priests, for such private action may jeopardize a larger solution.

57. c. In speaking of the recognition of a Lutheran Ministry not ordained by bishops, we are not in any way challenging the age-old insistence on ordination by a bishop within our own church or covertly suggesting that it be changed. . . .

58. d. We do not wish our statment (no. 54) concerning the Lutherans to be thought applicable to others without further and careful consideration. . . .

59. e. We caution that we have not discussed the implications that a recognition of valid Ministry would have for intercommunion or eucharistic sharing. . . .

Appendix II

Report of the Joint Lutheran/Roman Catholic Study Commission on "The Gospel and the Church" (abbreviated as "Malta Report")

The understanding of apostolic succession

57. The basic intention of the doctrine of apostolic succession is to indicate that throughout all historical changes in its proclamation and structures, the church is at all times referred back to its apostolic origin. The details of this doctrine seem to us today to be more complicated than before. In the New Testament and the early fathers, the emphasis was obviously placed more on the substance of apostolicity, i.e., on succession in apostolic teaching. In this sense the entire

church as the *ecclesia apostolica* stands in the apostolic succession. Within this general sense of succession, there is a more specific meaning: the succession of the uninterrupted line of transmission of office. In the early church, primarily in connection with defense against heresies, it was a sign of the unimpaired transmission of the gospel and a sign of unity in the faith. It is in these terms that Catholics today are trying once again to develop a deeper understanding of apostolic succession in the ministerial office. Lutherans on their side can grant the importance of a special succession if the preeminence of succession in teaching is recognized and if the uninterrupted line of transmission of office is not viewed as an *ipso facto* certain guarantee of the continuity of the right proclamation of the gospel.

58. It can also be of ecumenical importance to indicate that the Catholic tradition knows of individual instances of the ordination of priests by priests which were recognized as valid. It still needs to be clarified to what extent this leaves open the possibility of a presbyterial succession.*

*(Footnote 32) Cf. C. Baisi, *Il Ministro straordinario degli ordini sacramentali* (Rome: 1935); Y. Congar, *Heilige Kirche* (Stuttgart: Schwabenverlag, 1966), pp. 285-316; P. Fransen, in *Sacramentum Mundi*, IV, 1969, col. 1270f; W. Kasper, "Zur Frage der Anerkennung der Ämter in den lutherischen Kirchen," in *Theol. Quartalschrift* (Tübingen), Vol. 151, pp. 97-109.

* * *

The possibility of a mutual recognition of the ministerial office

63. The Catholic participants are convinced in view of recent biblical and historical insights as well as on the basis of the ecumenical experience of the working of the Holy Spirit in other churches, that the traditional rejection of the validity of the Lutheran ministerial

office must be rethought. The recognition of the ecclesial character of other church communities, as expressed by Vatican II,* can be, theologically speaking, interpreted as a first step toward the recognition of the ministerial offices of these churches. Also worthy of note is the point that the ministerial office arose in Lutheran churches through a spiritual break-through in an emergency situation. Reconsideration of the doctrine of apostolic succession and reflection on ministries of charismatic origin as well as on presbyterial succession seem to permit a correction of the traditional point of view. Therefore, the Catholic members request the appropriate authorities in the Roman Catholic Church to consider whether the ecumenical urgency flowing from Christ's will for unity does not demand that the Roman Catholic Church examine seriously the question of recognition of the Lutheran ministerial office.

*(Footnote 36) Cf. Decree on Ecumenism, 3f; 19.

4.
Recommendations From LED II

The Report of the Lutheran-Episcopal Dialogue I (LED I) in the U.S.A. was subtitled "Exploration and Progress." Representatives of these two great ecclesiastical communities, which have a common heritage from the sixteenth century Reformation, similar styles of church life and liturgical worship, reverence for the catholic tradition, but only sporadic moments of historical interaction, came together to get better acquainted with one another and to determine whether there was sufficient commonality to work toward closer relationships. The Report of LED I found substantial areas of agreement by comparing the respective requirements for intercommunion/pulpit and altar fellowship in the Chicago-Lambeth Quadrilateral and Article VII of the Augsburg Confession. While not recommending full pulpit and altar fellowship between the Protestant Episcopal Church in the U.S.A. (PECUSA) and the three participating Lutheran Church bodies (ALC-LCA-LCMS), the dialogue panel did recommend limited intercommunion between parishes or congregations "subject to the consent of the appropriate local authorities."

The LED I recommendations were not widely circulated among the membership of the respective churches and the hoped-for developments in the Lutheran-Episcopal relationships did not occur on any broad basis. We believe a number of factors account for this apparent lack of implementation. During the years 1972-76, the church bodies represented in the dialogue focused their attention on other issues; for example, within the Episcopal Church: the ordination of women to the priesthood, the revision of the Book of Common Prayer, and the study of and response to the national and international dialogues with the Roman Catholic Church; within the Lutheran Church-Missouri Synod: the question of the ordination of women, the formation of Seminex and the separation of AELC; for Lutherans generally: the new Lutheran Book of Worship and Lutheran involvement in Roman Catholic-Lutheran dialogue on both national and international levels.

Because of the lack of wide distribution and study, the LED I recommendations were misunderstood or seen as too radical and/or inconsistent with the doctrine and practice of the participating churches; for example, some felt that the recommended interim eucharistic fellowship was at odds with the approaches followed in other dialogues and that all dialogues needed to be consistent with each other; many felt the need for more historical and theological documentation of the recommendations; others questioned the apparent interchangeability of Lutheran "confessionalism" with Anglican "historic episcopate" as a form of apostolicity.

Certain things have transpired in the meantime both among Lutherans and Episcopalians which affect our relationship; some of them are:

1. In 1976 the Joint Commission on Ecumenical Relations (now the Standing Commission on Ecumenical Relations) of the Episcopal Church adopted a restatement of Apostolicity which moved in the direction of broader interpretation.*

2. The 1976 General Convention of the Episcopal Church adopted "Guidelines for Interim Eucharistic Fellowship" with the churches of the Consultation on Church Union. The Convention also, as had several previous General Conventions, reaffirmed the Chicago-Lambeth Quadrilateral as the basis for ecumenical dialogue with other Christian bodies.

*See The Report of The Joint Commission on Ecumenical Relations to the 65th General Convention of the Episcopal Church, 1976.

3. In 1977 the Lutheran (ALC, AELC, LCA) and Episcopalian (Dioceses of Michigan and Western Michigan) judicatory heads in Michigan adopted a statement "Free to Share" on the basis of the 1972 LED I recommendations. More recently in Massachusetts, Lutheran and Episcopal parishes have received approval from regional church authorities for joint celebrations of the eucharist on "special ecumenical occasions."

4. The 1978 Ecumenical Consultation of the Episcopal Church (Detroit) urged an "intensified dialogue" with Lutherans because the 1977 Episcopal Diocesan Ecumenical Officers survey disclosed that the Lutheran-Episcopal dialogue ranked second (after the Anglican-Roman Catholic Conversations) on the list of priorities among Episcopalians.

5. In 1978 the Lambeth Conference passed a resolution encouraging Anglican churches "to give special attention to our ecclesial recognition of the Lutheran Church on the basis of" the Anglican-Lutheran International Conversations (the Pullach Report, 1972), resolution 2 of the second meeting (Dublin, 1973) and resolution 5 of the third meeting (Trinidad, 1976) of the Anglican Consultative Council.

6. In 1978 the LCA and ALC adopted a new statement on "Communion practices," which provides guidelines for sharing the sacrament with baptized Christians of other churches.

7. The 1979 General Convention of the Episcopal Church adopted a new resolution and commentary on "Eucharistic Sharing," a statement of a "Goal for Visible Unity" and passed a resolution calling for "intensified dialogue with the Lutherans."

8. The 1978 Lutheran Book of Worship and the 1979 Book of Common Prayer share a similar structure for the Eucharistic Liturgy, similar material for the daily prayer offices, a common use of the historic church year, many

of the same lesser festivals and commemorations, the three-year lectionary for Sundays and festivals, the two-year daily lectionary, the same translation of the Psalter, many of the same collects, and a use of texts translated by the International Consultation on English Texts for Creeds, Lord's Prayer, and canticles.

As a result of our studies and discussions in LED II:

A. We, the PECUSA, AELC, ALC, and LCA participants, are able to affirm the recommendations of LED I and move beyond them in recommending the following:

1. That our respective Church bodies "mutually recognize" one another as true churches where the Gospel is truly preached and the sacraments duly celebrated (cf. Article XIX of the Articles of Religion, Augsburg Confession, Article VII) by taking appropriate legislative action.

2. That, because of the consensus achieved in the discussions of LED I and II on the chief doctrines of the Christian faith, our respective churches work out a policy of interim eucharistic hospitality so that Episcopalians may be welcomed at Lutheran altars and Lutherans may be welcomed at Episcopalian altars.

3. That the kind of joint worship recommended in the Report of the International Lutheran-Anglican Conversations be authorized and encouraged: "In places where local conditions make this desirable, there should be mutual participation from time to time by entire congregations in the worship and eucharistic celebrations of the other church. Anniversaries and other special occasions provide opportunity for members of the two traditions to share symbolic and eucharistic worship together."

4. That our church bodies take steps to cooperate in the publication and circulation of the reports and recommendations of LED I and LED II and other materials designed to popularize in the churches the findings of these dialogues.

5. That our respective church bodies encourage Episcopalian and Lutheran congregations to covenant together on the local level for the purpose of such things as: (a) mutual prayer and mutual support; (b) common study of the Holy Scriptures and the materials of LED I and LED II; (c) participation of Lutheran and Episcopal clergy at one another's services on special occasions; and (d) joint programs of religious education, theological discussion, mission, evangelism and social action.

6. That a third series of Lutheran Episcopal dialogues be held, with an emphasis on the means and models for implementing LED I and LED II, including such doctrinal discussions as may be pertinent. Discussion should focus on a mutually accepted order for ministry, with attention given to the role and office of bishop, diaconal ministry and the ministry of the laity.

B. We, the LCMS participants, recommend the following:

1. that we urge our constituent church bodies to publish and circulate the agreed statements for local discussion and dialogue among local pastors and parishes of the respective bodies for information, edification, reaction, and mutually agreed-upon action;

2. that the unresolved issues listed in the documents calling for further amplification and clarification be commended to LED series III on the national level as well as to local dialogues urged above;

3. that we give thanks to God individually and corporately for His gift to us of one Lord, one faith, one Baptism, one God and Father of us all, even as we continue to pray that "all they who call upon your holy Name may come to agree in the truth of your holy Word and live in unity and godly love".

A Statement From Episcopalians to Episcopalians

As we survey our ten years of discussion between the major Lutheran bodies and the Episcopal Church, we give thanks for the growing appreciation, understanding, and admiration which those of us on the Episcopal representative team have experienced with reference to the Lutheran tradition and the Lutheran Churches of this country. What might have been clear to us from our study of church history has been made evident in our experience. The Lutheran tradition, being one of the conservative reformation bodies, stands very close to our own Anglican experience and understanding. While there can be little doubt that Anglicans and Lutherans have their own distinctive style and ethos, a careful appraisal of this report and its predecessor, series I, should make it clear that the fundamental affirmations of the Christian faith and essential ingredients of the Christian corporate life and individual life are to be found in both traditions. This is evidenced in particular by the theological agreement stated in the international discussions and also by the joint statements (on justification, eucharistic presence, Gospel, Scripture, and apostolicity) found in this report.

In light of our agreement, the question comes home to us Episcopalians: "What should we be doing about this?"

Perhaps it would not be amiss for us to take renewed note of the words of Christ in John's Gospel,

"I do not pray for these only but also for those who believe in me through their word, that they may all be one; even as thou, Father, art in me, and I in thee, that they also may be in us, so that the world may believe that thou has sent me." (John 17:20,21)

Pertinent also are the words of the Apostle:

"I therefore a prisoner for the Lord beg you to lead a life worthy of the calling to which you have been called, with all lowliness and meekness, with patience, forebearing one another in love, eager to maintain the unity of the Spirit in the bond of peace. There is one body and one spirit just as you were called to one hope that belongs to your call, one Lord, one faith, one baptism, one God and Father of us all, who is above all and through all and in all." (Ephesians 4:1-6)

Our ecumenical imperative rests on the *fact* that there is but one Body and one Lord and one Spirit and one faith; this oneness needs to be manifested in so far as possible visibly in the Church's life and witness. Its urgency also is related to our witness; the unity of the Church displayed to the world is a compelling evidence of the reconciling power of the Gospel. When Episcopalians and Lutherans have discovered such profound unity in the faith and life of the Gospel, our calling is to take the steps which will manifest our unity in Christ and which will give more adequate visible expression to that unity.

We do well to underline the recommendations of this second series of discussion. First, the recommendations from this round suggest that we take the necessary steps to mutually recognize one another as sister churches where the Gospel is truly preached and the sacraments duly celebrated, (Article XIX; Augustana 7). This step was also urged upon us by the last Lambeth Conference; we were asked "to give special attention to our ecclesial recognition of the Lutheran Church." In addition to this, it is urged that we share with one another at the Lord's table, both in the form of guest communion in which Lutherans are particularly invited to the table of the Lord as presided over by Episcopalians, and Episcopalians invited to eucharistic celebrations presided over by Lutheran pastors, and also in the form of congregational exchanges on special occasions when it would be appropriate. Naturally, these acts are not to happen in a vacuum, hence there is a strong recommendation that we in our congregations make use of these reports and joint statements so that we are informed more fully of one another; the best usage no doubt would be to discuss these things together in joint study groups and also to engage in joint study of scripture. This could lead us to put the Lund principle to work, "that we do everything together which we can do practically and in good conscience" so that we come to know each other through common worship, joint edification, and cooperation in mission. It is both appropriate and urgent for Lutheran and Episcopalian congregations to covenant together to come to know each other in this fashion whenever possible.

Having said the above, which is both exciting and urgent, it should be made clear that this report does not envision an institutional merger of the Lutheran and Episcopal Church or a full integration of ordained ministries. Episcopalians would want to insist that we hold the historic Episcopate not only joyfully for ourselves but for the wider and uniting church. Such a purpose and plan for full union is being discussed in the Consultation on Church Union but it is not being discussed between Lutherans and Episcopalians. One of the recommendations of this report is that a third series be established which would take up this whole question of a "mutually accepted order for ministry" which would discuss the ordained ministry in the context of the diaconal ministry, the role and office of the Bishop, and of the ministry of the laity. This third series, however should not be conducted as if Series One and Two had not taken place and as if recommendations of a far reaching and serious nature were not offered and responded to at the conclusion of the Second Series. Series Three will surely take place in the context of an increased sharing together of our life and mission in Christ and in the context of mutual recognition that we are both churches in which the Gospel is truly preached and the sacraments duly celebrated.

May these findings and this urgent call be heard by us all.

A Statement By Lutherans To Lutherans

The Lutheran-Episcopal Dialogue II has been a process of discovery and convergence. Our convergence on doctrinal matters is expressed in the joint statements and recommendations included in this report. But we have also discovered one another as friends in Christ and have grown to appreciate the spiritual treasures of each other's Churches.

We Lutheran participants in this dialogue have especially grown to appreciate the gift which the historic episcopate bestows on the church. We are aware of the distrust with which many American Lutherans regard the episcopate, especially in its aristocratic model, including negative experiences within the Lutheran family.

However, in spite of what many would regard as the retention of certain ceremonial trappings from the Middle Ages, the constitutional episcopate in PECUSA bears no relationship to the medieval "divine right" episcopate. In one of our study sessions we observed many similarities between the ways in which Episcopal and Lutheran bishops/presidents exercise their offices.

While it is incumbent upon all pastors to emulate apostolic example and exercise episcopal responsibility in matters of doctrine and practice, those who hold offices of judicatory leadership in the church have been especially regarded as a sign of apostolic succession because of their wider responsibilities in, with, and for the church. A "Declaration of Apostolic Succession," issued in 1958 by the United Lutheran Church in Germany, noted "the separation from the papalistic formulation of the succession" which occurred at the time of the Reformation for the sake of the Gospel, and declared that break to be "correct and necessary." Nevertheless, the statement asserted that episcopal succession may be "appropriate" even if it is not "necessary" for the *esse* of the church (Erklärung zur Apostolischen Sukzession," in *Informationsdienst der Vereinigten Evangelisch-Luther-ischen Kirche Deutschlands,* 1958, pp. 6, 12).

Because of what episcopal succession has meant to the church throughout much of its history, and because of its ecumenical significance today, we recommend that the Lutheran Churches in America begin an internal study of the historic episcopate to determine whether it is a viable form of ministry for our Churches. Our report notes that the Lutheran Confessions show a preference for the historic episcopate where and when that ministry can be maintained in the service of the gospel. We are also aware that the Lutheran Churches in Sweden, Finland, and some Lutheran Churches in Africa have bishops in the historic succession. Indeed, the current President of the Lutheran World Federation, Bishop Josiah Kibira of the Northwest Diocese of the Evangelical Lutheran Church in Tanzania, is ordained into the historic episcopate. We are convinced that our willingness to deal seriously with this issue would be regarded as a most positive sign by our Episcopalian brothers and sisters, could serve the cause of church unity, and might redound to our own blessing.

Part II
Some Papers
Presented at
the Dialogue

How an Anglican does Theology
by Josiah Ogden Hoffman, Jr.

Theology, for our purposes here, is regarded as an activity of the Church, One, Holy, Catholic, and Apostolic. It is fellow-Christians addressing themselves to the study of God, Father, Son, and Holy Spirit, and to the relationship between this Triune God and the universe which he created — especially that part of that universe which lies within human experience. In this sense, theology is clearly and inescapably *anthropomorphic,* the product of our all-too-human minds and expressed in human, even earthly language. To do theology is to enter with radical faith into a life-long dialogue with God in which his creation continues in us and his grace sustains us. Doing theology is loving God with our minds and our hearts and our wills, in that community of the Spirit which calls Jesus Lord, and which seeks to make Him known as the Saviour of all mankind.

Anglicans, again for our purposes here, are to be understood as those peculiar Christians who look to the See of Canterbury as their ancient spiritual home and who are married, for better for worse, for richer for poorer, in sickness and in health, to that particular liturgical document known as *The Book of Common Prayer,* in its several different national and linguistic editions. We come in various sizes, shapes, and colors — and devotional styles which, in the family, are identified as High-and-crazy, Broad-and-hazy, and Low-and-lazy! Praise God, our life together is nothing but trouble and satisfaction, until we are parted by death.

How do Anglicans do theology? Let me count a few of the ways. *First,* we do theology *biblically,* our final authority being the Holy Scriptures of the Old and New Testaments, with the Apocrypha thrown in for good measure, not to be applied to estalish any doctrine, but (in the very Anglican phrases of Article VI of the Thirty-Nine Articles of 1571) to be "read for example of life and instruction of manners." In that same Article, we took a stand long ago which we still take, namely, that "Holy Scripture containeth all things necessary to salvation: so that whatsoever is not read therein, nor may be proved thereby, is not to be required of any man, that it should be believed as an article of the Faith, or be thought requisite primary source and data-bank, so to speak, and all of the clergy of the Church, as theologians, as teachers of the laity, make at their ordination the following public declaration: "I solemnly declare that I do believe the Holy Scriptures of the Old and New Testaments to be the Word of God, and to contain all things necessary to salvation." It is understood, of course, that for each ordinand, man or woman, these words carry particular and personal meanings known only to God, as it were.

As Anglicans we are committed to the view that the Bible, like other ancient literature, is — like creeds and confessions — a human product, historically conditioned and culturally limited. Its special theological status rests upon its being rooted and grounded in the work of God the Holy Spirit in the life and experience of the believing community of the Old and the New Israel. God speaks his word to us in Scripture, and our vocation is to read, mark, learn, and inwardly digest that Word, that by patience and comfort of it we might embrace and ever hold fast the blessed hope of everlasting life, which that same God has given us in our Saviour Jesus Christ. In the last analysis, our approach to the Bible is *soteriological:* our very salvation is seen to depend upon the revelation of God in Christ encountered in its hallowed pages. Percy Dearmer, a great Anglican pastoral theologian, called the Bible the

"Book of books, our people's strength,
   Stateman's, teacher's, hero's treasure,
Bringing freedom, spreading truth,
   Shedding light that none can measure:
Wisdom comes to those who know thee,
   All the best we have we own thee."

A lot more could, and perhaps, should be said about the biblical rootage of any thology which deserves to be called Anglican. But it surely should be mentioned that our commitment to the historical and critical method of biblical study, based as it is on the major findings of modern linguistic and archaeological research, is both *open-ended* and *open-minded* about those findings, in a truly scientific and empirical spirit. We are open to God's continuing self-disclosure, and we never cease to acknowledge that, at best, ". . . what we see now is like a dim image in a mirror. . . . What (we) know now is only partial." (I Corinthians 13:12, TEV)

A *second* way in which Anglicans do theology is *traditionally:* we are truly *conservative* when it comes to our sense of obligation about passing on and down what we have received from those who have come before us in a great and unbroken tradition of Christian faith and life in *Ecclesia Anglicana.* We love our heritage, and we are deeply and perpetually committed to seeing that it remains alive and well in the various segments of our scattered ecclesiastical family. In the words of the Chicago-Lambeth Quadrilateral of 1886/1888, we speak of ". . . the substantial deposit of Christian Faith and Order committed by Christ and his Apostles to the Church unto the end of the world, and therefore incapable of compromise or surrender by those who have been ordained to be its stewards and trustees for the common and equal benefit of all men." Familiar to all of us in this Lutheran-Episcopal Dialogue are the four parts of that sacred traditional deposit, parts which we continue to affirm are "essential to the restoration of unity among the divided branches of Christendom." To wit:

1. The Holy Scriptures of the Old and New Testament as the revealed Word of God.

2. The Nicene Creed as the sufficient statement of the Christian Faith.

3. The two Sacraments — Baptism and the Supper of the Lord — ministered with unfailing use of Christ's words of institution and of the elements ordained by Him.

4. The Historic Episcopate, locally adapted in the methods of its administration to the varying needs of the nations and peoples called of God into the unity of His Church.

Theologically, that is as traditional as we can get! These are the parameters within which we operate, and our *episcopoi* are here regarded (however generously) as learned, scholarly, well-informed experts who have both the right and the obligation to transmit to us who live below in the flatland world their best theological judgments, that we in turn, like them, might relate them to our daily life and work. We do not see it as our — or their — business to make up a new Faith but, rather, to pass on to succeeding generations the Faith which we have received,

67

continually up-dating it in the thought forms and patterns of an expanding universe of theological discourse. In *The Book of Common Prayer 1979* of the American branch of the Anglican Communion we have an excellent example of this characteristically Anglican way of attempting to make the traditional contemporary. It is a document entitled "An Outline of the Faith, commonly called the Catechism." The primary intention for it is that it be used by parish priests, deacons, and lay catechists as an outline for instruction. It is a topic-by-topic commentary on the historic Apostles' and Nicene Creeds and, though not meant to be a complete statement of belief and practice, it is hoped that it will serve as a "point of departure for the teacher." With a genuine concern for reaching out to the "world" of the natural and secular man and woman, a second use of the Outline is seen in providing "a brief summary of the Church's teaching for an inquiring stranger who picks up a Prayer Book." How very Anglican! We are not going to hit anyone on the head with our Party Line, but if they are curious enough to want to check us out theologically, we will be ready for them. This new catechism ranges far and wide, from Human Nature and The Old Covenant to The Christian Hope, passing through many other doctrinal cities and towns on the way, in the very traditional question and answer form for ease of reference.

Having identified Scripture and Tradition as hall-marks of our Anglican style of doing theology, we now turn to a *third* way we address ourselves to the study of God: Anglicans theologize *reasonably,* with confidence in the human capacity to exercise intelligence and reason in the pursuit of truth in all its unity and comprehensiveness. It is our "thing" to insist that we all share a need to "make sense" out of our lived experience. We are incurable rationalists in a valid and healthy way, and we are not afraid to deal with philosophical and existential questions in a serious attempt to correlate them with the theological answers of an on-going Christian Tradition. We have not produced, as have other communions in Christendom, a great line of systematic theologians, and, perhaps, more's the pity (as Stephen Sykes has painfully pointed out in his *The Integrity of Anglicanism*). But we have a noble line of able Christian apologists who have been proud to bear — as was Henry VIII before them! — the title of Defender of the Faith. We recognize that we can never make sense of God, nor can we ever get rid of the literally wonder-full mystery that continues to surround him. But we really want to master the art of wondering about him, and our minds are appreciated as God-given instruments in our ceaseless quest for the meaning of human existence in his terms. Our faith is forever seeking understanding, that our lives may be meaningfully and creatively lived with one another in his world. We hope that a "reasonable faith" is not a contradiction in terms; and though much of theological reasoning is admitted to be logically circular, we comfort ourselves with William Temple's assurance that circular arguments are all right as long as the circles are large enough! We insist on taking our brains to Church with us and we encourage our people to use them to their limit.

We do not regard theology and philosophy as mortal and perpetual enemies, as old Tertullian saw Jerusalem and Athens. Rather, we want the dialogue to continue unabated between them, that it might keep them both humble and charitable. In the phrase of Langmead Casserley, we speak of "Graceful Reason" with true affection, aware always of her capacity to seduce, yet keeping our theological wits about us, in a truly exciting game that we trust leads to a surer knowledge of God and of ourselves. We have a concern to be both intellectually honest and intellectually respectable, and we hold fast to the view that all knowledge is ultimately knowledge of

God. For us, the assumption of the unity of Truth frees us from the fear of scientific and sociological research, for we do believe in a God who wants us to discover everything we can about him and his universe, the desired end being truly responsible and truly human living. The bottom line: our theologians are gentlemen!

And now abideth Scripture, Tradition, and Reason, these three. In what some would claim is typically Anglican fashion, we stubbornly refuse to say which of them is the greatest! We give much lip service to the first, but when we do theology our efforts at harmony have a way of coming out in three-part form. That form, in effect, constitutes our *fourth* way of doing theology, and we call it *liturgy*. How do Anglicans most characteristically do theology? They do it *liturgically,* and *The Book of Common Prayer* is our *Summa Theologica,* to all intents and purposes. We are dyed-in-the-wool liturgical theologians. We say, if you cannot dramatize your theology in *Liturgy for Living* (the title of a book by our esteemed dialogical colleague, Louis Weil), then forget it! Since 1549 and through all of our checkered history, as Anglicanism has matured and reached the ends of the earth, the dearly beloved *BCP* has been our manual of devotion and our missionary handbook. Most of our most interesting family fights have been over this Book, saturated as it is with Holy Scripture, traditional theological formulae, and reasonable periodic attempts to keep it both rooted in history and in tune with whatever may be the times. This Book is also stained with the blood of martyrs like Thomas Cranmer and all who have followed in his train — and tried in vain to match his matchless English!

Yes, if you really want to catch Anglicans in the very act of doing theology, go to one of their worship services, bringing all of your wits and senses with you. Though the ceremonial action and the ritual words and their musical accompaniment may leave much to be desired in an artistic way, the total experience will be one of authentic encounter with our Anglican heritage. You will find us at our best and worst at the same time! Whether it be the Daily Offices of Morning and Evening Prayer, or the various Rites for the celebration of the Holy Eucharist, or any of the Pastoral Offices from Confirmation to the Burial of the Dead, you will find us having a ball doing theology liturgically: that is, addressing ourselves to God, hearing him address us, doing the work of God *(Opus Dei)* that we might do our daily work to his greater honor and glory. Corporate worship is the beating heart of the Anglican communion, as it is of all of the other branches of Christ's Church. Here the Anglican light shines most brightly. Here, at the Training Table of the Lord, through the means of grace provided by Word and Sacrament, we receive all that is needful for the doing of the many tasks to which God in Christ has called us; Theology, Mission, Biblical and Historical Study, Pastoral Care, Community Service. Here the broken-ness of our lives and relationships is healed, here the spiritual sources of our intellectual gifts are refreshed and renewed, here our wills are emboldened to be and to do what God would have us be and do. Here we learn what it means to be of good cheer, that God in Christ and in us and we in him might overcome the world.

This leads us to a fifth and final way of "doing theology" — a way which surely should be mentioned before we take leave of our subject. Anglicans continue to be concerned that theology be done *pastorally* and *particularly,* that as human beings in a world divided against itself and armed with ultimate weapons of destruction we might be helped to cope with soul-size problems in something approaching a reconciling and Christian manner. One dimension of a reconciliation theology is that of *liberation:* we sense a call to theologize

71

in the context of the daily struggle of human beings everywhere against poverty, injustice, oppression, and exploitation. Yet another dimension is that of *race:* so-called "Black Theology" is one of many attempts to appreciate in terms of God the beauty of the particular experiences of particular people of color, that the drama of our salvation in Christ might be acted out in technicolor and panavision. To do theology in this arena means to draw relevant data from psychology and sociology and anthropology and all of the so-called social sciences which can be brought face-to-face with the particularities of the uniquely Christian revelation of God in Christ. It is to tread on dangerous ground claimed by everyone and no one. It is to venture out into very deep water in what seems to be a very small boat.

Finally, with a bit of hesitation, Anglicans quite recently (in places like the United States and Canada) have broken with centuries-old Catholic-Orthodox tradition and begun to do theology in *feminist* terms: with a fair share of the courage to be and of the will to believe that it is God's will, men and women together are beginning to do theology in a thought world dominated by and permeated with male myths, male perspectives, male definitions, male language, and male power. Where traditional theologians have perhaps concerned themselves with abstract problems like that of suffering, "particularist" theologians involved in ministries of reconciliation must ask, "Why do *I* suffer — as a member of the Third World, or the Black Race, or the Female Sex? And what, in God's Name, can *I* do to stop from hurting?"

Our Anglican theological vocation is to venture to keep the many "varieties of (theological) experience" we have been discussing in some sort of balance. Our dominant concern is *mission:* "to know the Christ and to make him known." Our deepest roots are in the many centuries of our *past,* and we deeply love our heritage. We want others to share this love for our special brand of historical continuity and theological comprehensiveness. Our *present* reality is *ecumenical,* inter-national, inter-racial and inter-sexual. Anglicanism has long since ceased to be an English phenomenon. Our Anglican 5% of the world's Christians is scattered across the face of the whole earth, and our Communion is itself an ecumenical movement. Our future is, to a degree, uncertain, as all futures are. It may be that our vocation as Anglicans (as Stephen Bayne once suggested) is to disappear, as a river disappears when it flows into a larger and deeper sea. The vision of a "coming great Church" — so dearly held by a previous generation of ecumaniacs — may turn out to be but a dream in the minds of men and women, rather than a master plan in the mind of God. Doubtless *God* knows *what* he is doing theologically — and *how* he is doing it! He has forever to complete his purposes for us and for the world. For Anglicans, as for all Christians, our assurance is that ". . . neither death, nor life . . . nor things present, nor things to come . . . shall be able to separate us from the love of God, which is in Christ Jesus our Lord." (*Romans* 8:38-9, KJV)

How a Lutheran Does Theology:
Some Clues from The Lutheran Confessions
by Robert W. Bertram

1. Lutheran theology begins where all Christian theology does, indeed where all Christian ministry does, namely, with our risen Lord's commissioning his followers to go — not alone but with him — to baptize and teach all nations until he closes this age. Theology, over and over again, is for that one interim teaching mission.

2. But aren't the two, theology and mission, too far apart for that? Isn't theology back here, in seminaries

73

and classrooms and libraries and studies? And isn't mission out there, out in the world? Doesn't mission mean being sent, sent out, out and away? And doesn't out-and-away entail distance, separation from the home base? It does. But then that is why doing theology, whatever else that means, means keeping the Word coming from headquarters to field — from Sender to sent. Mission threatens to interpose gaps which theology in turn must continually labor to straddle. Theology in that sense is trans-mission.

3. The gap, however, is not a geographical gap between out there and back here. Theological distance is not measured from, say, some seminary classroom as the point of origin. The origin is the Sender. The distant mission field, whether that be across the seas or downtown or just as likely on the seminary campus, is as distant theologically as it is distant from the Commissioner. The gap is between the world, whither he sends us, and himself. And that is the gap which theology strives to bridge.

4. That gap, the Christ-gap, has two dimensions (so to speak): horizontal and vertical. Horizontally there is a time gap. Our mission-Sender, an itinerant rabbi of the first century Middle East, did what he did — died and rose and sent his Spirit — then and there, once upon a time. But his times, alas, are no longer ours. Still, it was out here, out into this utterly different future, that he sent us. How to bridge that generations gap of almost 2000 intervening years of the most drastic historical change? By what possible transmission can his message get from his ancient world to our very different one without serious loss of meaning?

5. Then, as though that weren't enough, there is also a vertical gap: the gap between our Sender's message and the incredulity which his message perennially

evokes. Always it does. That credibility gap, his *skandalon,* is not a problem of historical distance. That gap was as prevalent in the days of our Sender and of his first apostles as it is (and had better be) today. Both gaps, the gap of time and the gap of unbelief, are the responsibility of theology to surmount. Thanks to the distant mission, distant from himself, on which he sent us.

6. Consider the horizontal gap first, that gap of which our historically and hermeneutically minded age is so poignantly aware. It was a gap of which even the Lutheran confessors in the sixteenth century were beginning to be aware. Indeed it was because of their gap — the gap in time between the prophets and apostles, on the one hand, and the later ages of the church, on the other — that confessions and creeds were deemed necessary at all. They were devices, just as "doing theology" is, for closing the historical distance between now and the New Testament. The theological "writings of ancient and modern teachers" show how "the doctrine of the prophets and apostles was preserved in post-apostolic times [*nach der Apostel Zeit*]," "setting forth how at various times [*jederzeit*] the Holy Scriptures were understood in the church of God by contemporaries [*von den damals Lebenden*] . . . ." That is likewise what the Lutheran Confessions themselves are, "the symbol of our time [*dieser Zeit*]." They are the original Christian faith so expounded as to fit "the schism in matters of faith which has occurred in our times [*zu unsern Zeiten*]." (*Formula of Concord,* Epitome, Preface)

7. Lutherans believe that these confessional testimonies of the sixteenth century, like the ecumenical creeds centuries before, faithfully crossed the horizontal gap between the bygone times of their Sender and the much later time of their own mission. These

confessors seem to us to have discovered the secret of "doing theology" for their "times," well enough to make us wish to learn their secret for times like our own.

8. Then do these post-biblical confessions, these subsequent doings of theology, introduce something different from their own "times" which was not in the Scriptures originally? Yes, indeed. Or if not something different, then at least something additional, something from a later history which the prophets and apostles themselves had not yet encountered. For if all that the confessions did was merely to duplicate what the Scriptures had already said, then what need would there be to add confessions? What need to continue "doing theology"? What need to cross the horizontal gap? Indeed, what horizontal gap?

9. The fact is, times change. And not only do the times change, and not even only languages — say, from Aramaic to Greek to Latin to German. If that were all, then the changes could be handled simply by new Bible translations. No, changing times bring also new problems or, if they were not altogether new, then at least the same old problems in new form. Paul, for example, never had to cope with Arius or with the medieval system of merit, certainly not in those forms. Could he even have imagined such distortions? Much less could he foresee how those distortions would arise out of his own doctrine? Really, it was only because Paul came first that these later abberations could invoke his support as they did. They were "Christian" heresies. That explains why "the ancient church formulated symbols:" because "immediately after the time of the apostles — in fact, already during their lifetime — false teachers and heretics invaded the church." (*Ibid.*) From then on

the invasions never stopped coming, no two of them ever quite the same. Because the church, which is Christ's mission, confronts always new and un-anticipated mission challenges, it must by "doing theology" relate the message of its Sender anew to each challenge in all its historic particularity. The horizontal gap expands apace. And so, lest the mission of Christ be outstripped, must theology.

10. Comes now a danger. Given the confessional symbols, which admittedly restate the original faith in a new and later idiom, the church is then tempted to misconstrue those symbols as a substitute for the biblical original. Restatement becomes displacement. Confessional theologies, hammered out for the needs of their own mission situations, are thus detached from the mission's origin. Of course, no proper confession or confessional theologian ever wants to say anything which was not first, at least implicitly, in the Scriptures themselves. Lutherans generally still agree, the only subscribable confession is one which is always *nach Anleitung Gottes Worts* (*Ibid.*, title), and "every doctrine should submit to this guidance [*nach dieser Anleitung*]." (*Ibid.*, 6; my translation) And for many of us, at least, it makes sense to subscribe the Lutheran Confessions confessionally at all, not "insofar as" (*quatenus*) they reflect the biblical Word but "because" (*quia*) they do.

11. Still, that very *quia* in turn can now misfunction, ironically, to displace the Scriptures. Exactly because our confession witnesses only to "the doctrine of the prophets and apostles," therefore the misimpression arises that their doctrine and our confession are indistinguishable. But if so, there would have been no need for the Reformers to bridge the horizontal gap. For then there would have been no such gap. In that case it is as though between the first century and the

77

sixteenth nothing had happended. What is worse, the whole point of the Preface of the Formula of Concord is lost, namely, "the distinction [*der Unterschied, discrimen*] between the Holy Scripture of the Old and New Testaments and all other writings." (*Ibid.*, 7) What comes to be forgotten, at least in practice, is that "Holy Scripture remains the only *Richter, Regel und Richtschnur*" — the three R's! — and that, in the theological courtroom, only Scripture is the "judge" and the confessions merely "witnesses" (*Zeugen*). (*Ibid.*, 7.8.2) To be sure, the *Unterschied* between Scripture and all other writings is not merely an *Unterschied* of time, as though the only distinction between them were that the former is early and the latter late. The horizontal gap does not exhaust their difference. But neither can their real difference be substantiated without that essential dimension, their historical distance.

12. Deprived of that wide historical *Unterschied* between Scripture and their own much later expositions of it, the confessors are then deprived of their boldness as well. And bold they were. When they submitted their confession, they did not arbitrarily fling it down saying, Here it is, take it or leave it. That unsure of themselves they were not. Rather they opened their books to public audit, calling upon any and all to check them out — against the Scriptures. Any and all who? "All nations," even "future generations" — "before God and among all nations, present and future" — and at the end of history, "Christ." (*Apology,* Preface, 15, 19; IV, 398; XIV, 5; and *passim*) In face of that daring invitation to examine their biblicalness, we do the confessions small credit when we say in effect, Oh that's all right, we'll take your word for it. It is precisely the theologian who subscribes them *quia* who accepts their invitation,

over and over. That is the mark of a fearless subscription. And it is the only way to appreciate how successfully the confessors did return all the way to their Sender and back once more to their own remote mission territory. The distance was far. But the trans-mission, they were sure, had connected. That is why they could afford to be so openly accountable. We begrudge them that, and we minimize their achievement, when we obscure the historical *Unterschied.*

13. How do confessions supplant Scripture in practice? Well, the obvious way would be to lay Scripture aside and to content oneself with the confessions exclusively. But that, if it is a danger at all, is a danger for only a few of us. Frankly, as post-seminary reading, the Lutheran Confessions are not all that popular. However, there is another, less obvious way. And that is to read Scripture itself anachronistically, as though it might just as well be a document from the sixteenth century Reformation, as though it had presented from the outset those later credal and confessional theologies obviously and ready-made. Such exegesis does indeed read the confessions into Scripture rather than out of it, hence unconfessionally, and sooner or later falsifies also the confessions, let alone Scripture. All because the horizontal gap, the historical distance, between Scripture and all other writings is underplayed. As a consequence it becomes harder and harder to recognize those historical circumstances native only to Scripture itself, and to recover its original genius. This, in turn, impairs Scripture's peculiar control, its *Anleitung,* of "all other writings."

14. With such anachronistic exegesis the long biblical trans-mission across the chasm from its ancient missionary origins to the most alien and far-flung

mission futures, loses its wonder. Then, though we may still speak respectfully of Scripture as the only "rule," the exclusive *regula,* what escapes us is the marvel of how this Word of God has in fact "ruled" down through history, not above and beyond the flux of time but directly through that flux and by means of it; how that Word has "regulated" to its own purpose the most obstreperous opponents and such bizzare notions as *homoousios* and *Trinitas;* how that same Word could still raise up from a disintegrating Christendom "a summary formula and pattern [*Begriff und Form*], . . . the summarized doctrine . . . drawn together out of the Word of God" (*Formula of Concord,* SD, "Summary Formulations, etc.," 1); how that *Begriff und Form* of the biblical Word — that constant, transhistorical shape of the faith, which is "the pure doctrine of the Word of God" (*Ibid.*) — never is "pure" if by that we mean divested of history but is always inextricably inter-twined with now this history, now that; how such historical versatility of the Word is, far from embarrassing, our very opportunity. It is, in short, the clue for engaging that trans-mission of the Word for also this, its most recent mission challenge: our times.

15. What all that presupposes, however, is that we first appreciate, without anachronism, the historic unique-ness of the biblical "prophets and apostles" and, before them, the uniqueness of their Sender. Well suited to such appreciation of the mission's origins is the method of modern historians or, as we have come to call it, the historical-critical method. Historians of Scripture do indeed exercise criticism. What they criticize, as well they might, are those anachronistic interpolations and accretions which later ages of the church have since read back into Scripture, as

though they had always been patently there. Here the historians, armed with their critical edge, are under obligation to do the negative thing and to protest: No, that is *not* what Galatians means, not yet it doesn't, not here in the time of its authorship.

16. Of course, biblical historians might also protest too much. They might turn reactionary and say, Galatians dare never mean anything more than what its author consciously intended by it. That sort of historical criticism is obscurantist, for it forgets that Galatians still had a long and varied career ahead. For that subsequent career the original epistle, as it stood, was already well equipped with the most versatile, future implications. But the historian is right, those implications are always controlled by what the document meant at the outset. In any case, at the time of Galatians' origin most of its implications were still future and unforeseeable. And it is the way of the Word to take history in stride as and when it comes. Theology consists, in part, in waiting and watching for that stride. But how, without the methods of history? They are indispensable for "doing theology" across the horizontal gap, to bring the Sender's message ungarbled to this present farthest reach of his mission.

17. Speaking of historical-critical exegesis, we are reminded of that most notorious charge levelled against its practitioners, most often undeservedly: namely, that they criticize not only the history which later, anachronistic theologians have read back into Scripture but also that very history which occurs right within Scripture and which Scripture cannot do without. For instance, the biblical history of our Lord's resurrection.

18. And this reminder from historical criticism recalls, in turn, that second gap which "doing theology"

confronts: the vertical gap — the perennial and universal gap of an unbelief which is scandalized by the gospel. That credibility gap, even more oppressively than the horizontal gap of historical distance, afflicts Christ's mission wherever and whenever it touches the world. So here too, if his mission is to span this gap as well, theology must serve as trans-mission.

19. But back up a moment. What was the connection, just alluded to, between the historical criticism of biblical events and the vertical gap of unbelief? The connection between them is not at all obvious. The obvious explanation would be that the two things are identical: historical criticism and unbelief. At first glance, radical criticism of Scripture's history appears to be a clear case of unbelief, plain and simple. Now unbelief it may be, though not plain and simple. There is a popular myth about unbelievers. Unbelievers supposedly deny Jesus' resurrection for the simple reason that it is extraordinary: ordinarily people who die stay dead, Jesus died, ergo he stayed dead. At least that is why unbelievers are *assumed* to deny the resurrection, namely, because it violates the uniformity of nature, or the historicist principle of analogy. As unbelief, that would indeed be plain and simple.

20. But does that explanation of unbelief really suffice, obvious though it seems? If that is all that drives people to discount biblical history, then why all the grand talk about their being scandalized by the gospel? After all, what is scandalous about the gospel is not only our Lord's resurrection but prior to that, says Paul, his crucifixion. Still, only a few eccentrics disbelieve that. Offhand, a crucifixion is not really that extraordinary — that is, not unless there is something about unbelievers themselves which made both crucifixion *and* resurrection *necessary*! But

then that is what taxes people's credulity: not Jesus' rising as such, nor his dying, but rather our own need of them — our need of him. Disbelieving *that* does not stem from historical criticism. People disbelieve an incredible historical claim not merely because it is unusual but also because there seems to be no need which requires such unusual happenings. Jesus' resurrection is not only extraordinary, it seems unwarranted — unwarranted by anything in your situation and mine. But once you add that, then even Jesus' resurrection is not only extraordinary, it seems unwarranted — unwarranted by anything in your situation and mine. But once you add that, then even Jesus' crucifixion is unbelievable. That unbelief is the vertical gap. And it is that unbelief, not historical criticism, which "doing theology" must overcome.

21. Once again the Lutheran Confessions provide precedent. In the Apology of the Augsburg Confession, especially in Article IV, a recurrent counter-argument against the Roman *Confutatores* is that the latter render Christ "unnecessary." Not that they deny Christ's *historia*. (What good Catholic would ever deny that!) On the contrary, they affirm it all, including every last assertion of the Nicene-Chalcedonian christology, as the signatories of the Augustana of course did, too. The trouble, though, with the Roman accusers was that they denied the biblical *sola fide*. And it was that denial of theirs, presumably, which obviated any need of Christ. For all their high-flown christological subscription, their actual, working soteriology did not in fact make "use" of that Christ. It let him go to waste — or let him, as Paul said, die in vain — as though he had never needed to exist at all. After that it is immaterial; at least theologically immaterial, what you believe about his history.

83

22. Accordingly, the highest criterion of "doing theology" is so to do it as to show the need of Christ. It is not enough to affirm him, no matter how biblically. Theologies which are merely nominally Christian can do that. No, everything depends on whether those theologies, in all they say, can show cause for Christ's coming as he came and doing as he did. Failing that, all their other assertions about his *historia* reduce to mere *fides historica,* which in itself is a form of unbelief.

23. This staggering demand upon theology — and every preacher can sympathize with how staggering it truly is — would in our day fall particularly upon that branch of theology called systematics. It may well be, therefore, that the modern historical mind is encouraged in its unbelief of biblical history, not just because biblical historians have failed to substantiate it but also because systematicians have failed intelligibly to show need of it. If so, that augments the already massive proof that "doing (systematic) theology" is especially in line for improvement, also within Lutheranism.

24. The Lutheran Confessions' "systematic" *par excellence* for showing the need of Christ, for "using" him in all his historicality, takes the form there of a hermeneutical procedure: the distinguishing and relating of Scripture's law and promise (or gospel). Not that Scripture itself always and explicitly distinguishes these two motifs. More often than not, perhaps, it does not. In fact, that may well be part of Scripture's special genius, namely, that it trans-mits (tradere) the legal and promissory streams of God's Word in such an already faithful coordination that it has no need of dividing them.

25. The "legal" dimension of the biblical Word is that which "commends good works" and, conversely,

criticizes their opposite. The "promissory" dimension is that which proffers the divine mercy because of Christ. If the question before the confessors at Augsburg was how to commend good work without sacrificing the promise, then their answer, as they knew, lay in the way Scripture kept *lex* and *promissio* in their native, God-intended balance. Promise, dominant; law, sub-dominant. Law, penultimate; gospel, ultimate. Both of them divine absolutes, yet with the promise always having the final word.

26. But then why must the distinction-compulsive theologian lay heavy hands upon the biblical harmonies, putting asunder what God has there seen fit to join together? The explanation, of course, lies not in the theologian's compulsions. And yet in a way it does, at that. For there is that compulsion, which is not unique to theologians but is the common affliction of religious people generally, or for that matter of all unbelievers. (And who, even among strong believers, is not also and simultaneously an unbeliever?) Call that compulsion, as the Augusburg Confession's Apology does, the *opiniu legis.*

27. In the exegete this *opinio legis* works as a subversive bias, spoiling the native rationale of biblical law and promise. As *opinio,* it is an illusion. But it is not merely illusion. It is illusion about something which in its own right is true, the biblical *lex.* The element of illusion comes when people, as they always are wont to do, accord that *lex* soteriological significance, the last word. The ensuing disaster is that the promise is displaced, "omitted" or, in actual effect, abandoned. But one might expect that in that case the *law* at least would survive intact. It does not. Left alone, without the promise to trump it, the *lex* would be just too threatening to be a credible way of salvation. So to preserve the illusion of its saving power, the legalist

85

scales also the law down reductionistically to barely a shadow of its old biblical self. Yet even in that truncated form it can still avenge itself upon its abuser in the twin forms of hypocrisy and despair.

28. Hence the most pressing reason for distinguishing Scripture's law and promise is not that these are always set apart as such in the biblical text, but rather that human unbelief insinuates into the reading of that text an alien *Vorverständnis,* with a resulting combination of law and promise which is downright unbiblical and, pastorally speaking, fatal. By contrast, the biblical ordering (*ordo*) of *lex* and *promissio* can afford — as best of all Jesus himself does — to reveal the law in all its original force, as *accusator,* removing the "veil of Moses" by which that law has otherwise (even in Scripture) had to be masked. Yet this full facing of the law in all its criticalness is impossible only because, in its assigned subordination, it is domesticated by the promise. But where, pray, does that happen? Where, if both wrath and mercy are God's own, do they become reconciled and so avoid an ultimate dualism? In one place: in Jesus the Christ, crucified and risen and, ever since, interceding for us on the basis of his historic deed. As a result the intimidating law, which still goes on accusing with perfect right, can now be lived with, even internalized and made use of — in the daily, penitential living out of our Baptisms and in losing ourselves for the world. And the final resolution of this New History is only a matter of time.

29. The upshot is that unbelief, the unbelief of the vertical gap, is taken with full seriousness. For, after all, it really is incredible — indeed, it is humanly impossible to believe — that the itinerant, first-century rabbi would "need" to go to such lengths to achieve the merciful mission of God toward us. But

once that is believed, as again and again it is, the believer can assimilate also the law, can take its criticism, and can even profit from it, advancing its commendable good work in society. Still, *lex* is always only proximate to Scripture's distinctive *promisso*. And only *promissio,* finally, is the solvent of the world's hard unbelief.

30. *Promissio* is the secret of *missio.* For the mission's Sender was himself the keeping of that promise. And the mission's gaps, across which we move with our theological doings, are ultimately spanned by the same promise — of himself by the Spirit through his Word.

The Authority of the Scriptures in Anglicanism
by Reginald H. Fuller

It is well known that the Anglican Reformation began as an act of state. When in 1532 Henry VIII set in motion the legislation which was to separate the Church of England from the jurisdiction of the Roman Pontiff and place it under the crown, the initial justification for this act was a political one: that "England is an empire." At this stage there was no intention to change in any way the doctrine of the mediaeval church. In 1534 for instance it was stated that there was an express intention not to depart from "the very articles and Catholic faith of Christendom."

Very soon, however, in fact in the same year (1534), Convocation found itself debating the scriptural basis for the repudiation of papal authority: "Whether the Roman Pontiff has any greater jurisdiction bestowed on him by God in the Holy Scripture in this realm of England than any other foreign bishop." Thus the Henrician reforms began to be justified by an appeal from existing customs and doctrines to Scripture, read in its literal and historical sense.

It was not long before other doctrinal matters began to be controverted. The influence of the continental reformation inevitably began to be felt in England. And for a time Henry's political interests drew him closer to the party of Reform. It was during this phase that the Ten Articles of Religion were expounded. Here a distinction was drawn for the first time between those things expressly commanded by God and necessary to salvation, and other matters not commanded by God or necessary to salvation, "yet being a long continuance for a decent order and honest policy, prudently instituted—and therefore to be observed."[1] In a treatment of purgatory these Articles opposed any interpretation that involved an addition to Scripture and the witness of the creeds.

In 1537 there appeared the Bishops' Book on *The Institution of a Christian Man*. This asserted for the first time the supremacy of Scripture, which it regarded *in toto* as the Word of God. This set the stage for the later reformation of doctrine, although this was about as far as that reformation was to proceed in Henry's reign.

The chief formulations of reformed Anglican doctrine are to be found in the successive editions of the English Book of Common Prayer (1549, 1552, 1559, 1662), the two books of Homilies (1547 and 1571) and the successive editions of the Articles of Religion, the Forty-two Articles of 1553 and the Thirty-nine Articles of 1563, revised 1571.

The Prayer Books since 1552 have included the Ordinal, which contains a question in the Ordering of Priests which is important for our subject:

> Be you perswaded that the holy scriptures conteine sufficiently all doctryne, required of necessity for eternall saluacion, through faith in Jesus Christ? And are you determined with the sayd scriptures to instructe the people committed to your charge, and to teache nothing (as required of necessitie to eternall saluacion) but that you shalbe perswaded, maye be concluded, and proued by the scripture?

In the *First Book of Homilies*, there is a homily entitled "A Fruitful Exhortation to the Reading and Knowledge of Holy Scripture." Its opening sentences read as follows:

> Unto a Christian man there can be nothing either more necessary or profitable than the knowledge of holy Scripture; forasmuch as in it is contained God's true word, setting forth his glory and also man's duty. And there is no truth or doctrine necessary for our justification and everlasting salvation, but that is or may be drawn out of that fountain and well of truth.

The second book of Homilies contains a homily entitled "An Information for them which take Offence at Certain Places of the Holy Scripture." It asserts a strong doctrine of inspiration, citing in support 2 Tim 3:16, 2 Pet 1:21, and John 16:13.

It also contains the statement:

> The Holy Scriptures are God's treasure house, wherein are found all things needful for us to see, to hear, to learn and to believe, necessary for the attaining of eternal life.

Turning now to the most explicit document on the authority of Scripture as held in Reformation Anglicanism, the Thirty-nine Articles, we find no less than six of them relate to the authority of Scripture, Articles VI, VII, VIII, XX, XXI, and XXXIV.

The most important is Article VI, which reads:

> Holy Scripture containeth all things necessary to salvation: so that whatsoever is not read therein, nor may be proved thereby, is not to be required of any man, that it should be believed as an article of the faith, or thought to be requisite or necessary to salvation.

This is followed by a statement on the Canon, which includes a complete listing of the OT books minus the Apcrypha, and a statement about the Apocrypha which reads:

> And the other books (as Hierome saith) the Church doth read for example of life and instruction of manners; but yet doth it not apply them to establish any doctrine . . .

This is followed by a list of the apocryphal books. Article VI closes with a statement that all commonly received books of the NT are accounted Canonical.

Article VII treats specifically with the Old Testament. It affirms that

> The Old Testament is not contrary to the New; for both in the Old and New Testament everlasting life is offered mankind in Christ.

The Article later on distinguishes between the ceremonies and rites of the Mosaic Law, which are not binding, and the civil precepts, which are not necessarily to be received in any commonwealth, and the moral commandments which are to be obeyed by all Christian men.

Article VIII deals with the three Creeds (the American version of 1801 cut out all reference to the Anthanasian Creed), and affirms that they ought thoroughly to be received and believed. The reason for this is that "they may be proved by most certain warrants of Holy Scripture."

Article XX, entitled "Of the Authority of the Church," recognizes that the Church has power to decree rites or ceremonies and also authority in matters of faith. However, this authority is limited by Scripture:

> Yet it is not lawful for the Church to ordain anything that is contrary to God's Word written. It may not expound one passage of Scripture so that is is repugnant to another.

Then the Church is defined in well-known words as a "witness and keeper of Holy Writ."

Article XXI, "Of the authority of General Councils," limits the authority of General (i.e., Eucumenical) Councils to affirming what Holy Scripture itself proclaims as necessary to salvation:

> Wherefore things ordained by them as necessary to salvation have neither strength nor authority, unless it may be declared that they be taken out of Holy Scripture.

Article XXIV, "Of the Traditions of the Church," really explicates Article XX on the authority of the Church. It claims that the Church has authority to ordain rites and ceremonies, so nothing be ordained against God's Word. It condemns those who impugn traditions and ceremonies "not repugnant to the Word of God," and claims for every particular or national church the right to ordain, change and abolish ceremonies and rites of merely human authority.

How are we to assess these Articles? To begin with it is clear from Article VI that they take their stand not merely on the primacy but on the supremacy of Scripture, that is the Reformation position of *sola scriptura.* Yet there is a certain ambivalence about the content of Scripture. Article VI suggests that it contains propositional truths which have to be believed for salvation, whereas Article VIII, the one about the Old Testament, suggests that the primary purpose of Scripture is to offer not a list of saving *credenda,* but everlasting life to mankind in Christ. Article VI is concerned with *fides quae creditur* and in this point related more closely to the stratum of the NT which scholars today refer to as early catholicism, whereas Article VII is in this respect truer to the Pauline-evangelical concept of faith. It sees the function of the Church not primarily as teaching saving truth, but as the proclamation of salvation through Jesus Christ. Here, perhaps, is one of the sources of two competing strands in Anglicanism, the catholic and evangelical. In later official documents, we shall see the catholic strand is paramount.

Article VII on the Creeds is carefully formulated so as not to suggest that the Creeds have an authority independent of Scripture. They are commended only because they may be proved by Scripture.

Such a position with regard to the Creeds was destined to prove inadequate. The Creeds would later be valued not merely because they are congruous with scripture, but more because they point to the center and core of the Christian faith.

The Article about the Councils (XXI) confines itself, similarly to the Article on the Creeds, to recognizing their authority only when they "ordain" as necessary to salvation things patently "taken out of Holy Scripture."

Two comments here are called for. First, it does not state which Councils the Articles have in mind. In the seventeenth century the first four Councils (Nicea I, Constantinople I, Ephesus, and Chalcedon) were generally specified, although some later Anglicans have argued for six or seven councils.[2] In effect, the four Councils mean the acceptance of the christological dogmas as is clear from Article II. The second point is that as with the Creeds no positive function is assigned by the Articles to the Councils. Later Anglicanism was to recognize that the conciliar definitions provide a hermeneutic principle for the interpretation of the Scriptures. The mainstream of Anglicanism has generally been suspicious of any exegesis or systematic Christology which appears to deny the credal and conciliar doctrine of the incarnation.[3]

All in all, one may say that the Thirty-nine Articles set the tone for future Anglicanism by its recognition of the primacy and supremacy of Scripture on the one hand, and yet prepared the way for a more diffuse conception of authority by the place given the Creeds, and the early Ecumenical Councils, by its claim as a national Church to ordain rites and ceremonies not contrary to God's word, and by its exercise of doctrinal authority in issuing the Articles. The claim of authority in the area of rites and ceremonies was exercised in the enactment of the Book of Common Prayer with its customary usages, such as kneeling communion, the surplice, the sign of the cross in baptism, and the use of the ring in marriage. In the 16th century this also included episcopacy. But the controversies in the seventeenth century were destined to lead Anglican theologians to move up episcopacy from the adiaphora to the level of the Creeds and Councils as part of the proper interpretation of Scripture. This was reflected in the 1667 Prayer Book, which added to the Preface of the Ordinal the rule requiring either episcopal ordination for ministers of other churches seeking to minister in the Church of England, or their ordination according to the English ordinal.

In 1571, the same year that the Articles were propounded in their final Reformation form, Convocation passed a Canon which stipulated that all preaching was to be agreeable to the teaching of the Old and New Testaments "and" to what the "catholic fathers and ancient bishops have collected from this self-same doctrine." Although this Canon never received the royal assent, and therefore lacked canonical force, it both registered a development of Anglican thinking and encouraged further development. In itself the statement is somewhat ambiguous. What does that "and" really mean? It certainly does not mean doctrine additional to that of the Scriptures for it is explicitly restricted to what the "catholic fathers and ancient bishops" have gathered from Scripture. But it certainly encourages the idea of the diffusion of authority, and the idea that antiquity (as 17th century Anglicans liked to call it) provides a hermeneutical key for the interpretation of Scripture. Yet the supremacy of Scripture remains.

Meanwhile Anglican apologetics against Rome produced considerable reflection on the basis for the instance on the supremacy of Scripture — a basis which the Articles do not provide. At least four reasons were offered in the 16th and 17th centuries for the scriptural principle: 1) Their self-evidencing quality (Rogers, Whitaker). 2) Their apostolic or near-apostolic authorship (Burnet). 3) The teaching of the fathers acknowledged the supremacy of Scripture. 4) Also, it is supported by the *testimonium Spiritus Sancti*. It is perhaps a shortcoming of the official doctrine of the Church of England at the Reformation that it had offered no apology for the supremacy of Scripture. But later there was cause to be thankful that it was never committed to a definition of the nature of inspiration or to a claim for the inerrancy of

Scripture. Thus the way was left open for the acceptance of critical methods in the latter part of the 19th century.

While in no sense an official theologian of the Church of England, Richard Hooker was widely influential in upgrading the importance of antiquity and reason in Anglican thought. The former is the hermeneutical context for the interpretation of Scripture, the latter is the necessary tool for exegesis. Hooker wrote: "exclude the use of natural reasoning concerning the Articles of our faith, and then that Scripture doth concern the Articles of our faith who can assure us?" The contemporary Church, he held, has authority to develop the implications of Scripture in order to apply its trackings to current issues in doctrine and morals. Thus it is interesting to find him going beyond Scripture in using natural law deduced by reason to condemn slavery. For Hooker, too, tradition provided the context for the interpretation of Scripture. Following Cranmer and Jewell, he attached considerable importance to the first four General Councils as a secondary authority. Tradition, however, he is clear, has only a relative authority. It is not absolute and infallible, like Scripture or even reason. While Scripture contains all things necessary to salvation, reason is necessary in order to ascertain the literal meaning of Scripture, which alone is authoritative. The fathers of the church are helpful, too, in exegesis.

Hooker thus goes further than the Articles in assigning a more distinct role to the secondary authorities. It is not simply that those secondary authorities concur with Scripture. It is rather that they offer the indispensable clue to its right understanding and application. This view of antiquity and reason was to have profound effects on Anglican theology during the 17th century, although the official documents of Anglican theology remained practically unchanged. It begins the process whereby the supremacy of Scripture is reduced to primacy.

But in 1628 the Articles were prefaced by "His Majesty's Declaration" which remained in the Church of England Prayer Books until 1975.[4] This was intended to allay Puritan controversies and the attempt of the Puritan clergy to rivet upon Anglican preachers the doctrines of the Synod of Dort. It is thought that the declaration was the work of Archbishop Laud. It affirmed that the Articles are not merely consonant with Scripture, but that they provide their hermeneutical key in contemporary controversies:

> The Articles of the Church of England . . . do contain the true Doctrine of the Church of England agreeable to God's Word . . .
>
> That therefore in these both curious and unhappy circumstances . . . we will, that all further curious search be laid aside, and these disputes shut up in God's promises, as be generally set forth to us in the Holy Scriptures, and the general meaning of the Articles of the Church of England, according to them. And no man shall hereafter either print or preach to draw the Article aside in any way, but shall submit to it in the plain and full meaning thereof; and shall not put his own sense or comment to be the meaning of the Article, but shall take it in the literal and grammatical sense.

The final phrase was to cause much controversy at the time of Newman's Tract XC (1841).

The other major consequence of the Anglican theological renaissance in the 17th century, as we have already noted, was the addition to the Preface to the Ordinal in 1662, requiring that ministers from other churches either have been previously ordained episcopally, or be ordained under the Anglican Prayer Book Ordinal before being allowed to exercise the office of priesthood in the Church of England. No official statement was made on whether this was merely a disciplinary rule, or whether it was enacted for doctrinal reasons. It was probably directed against Presbyterian ordinations in the commonwealth period, not against continental ordinations.[5] The non-Jurors after 1688, and the Tractarians after 1833, were to insist that it was doctrinal. Neither party would have regarded this as an addition to Scripture, but would have justified it on the ground that antiquity was the true interpreter of Scripture.

This brings us to the 19th century, which saw the Tractarian movement and the rise of biblical criticism. The Tractarians had no intention of abandoning the primacy of Scripture, but its supremacy became problematical. And they believed in its inspiration and inerrancy. But they shifted a great deal of weight from Scripture to Tradition, particularly to what they regarded as the consensus of the undivided Church. Their favorite slogan was that of St. Vincent of Lerins: *quod semper, quod unique, quod ab omnibus.* They became critical of the Reformation (Richard Hurrell Froude had said the Reformation was like a broken leg which had been set badly: it had to be broken again and reset). This meant interpreting the Thirty-nine Articles (which because of their deliberate inclusiveness could be patient of wide interpretation) in a sense agreeing with that of the consensus of antiquity — i.e., in what the Tractarians regarded as a Catholic sense. In this the Tractarians did not believe they were innovating within Anglicanism; they were re-implementing the position of the Caroline divines. But in effect they went further, for as we have seen, the Caroline divines had used the Articles in their literal and grammatical sense as a weapon against the Calvinists, whereas the Tractarians re-interpreted the Articles in a non-literal and non-grammatical sense to conform with antiquity. This tendency reached its climax in Newman's Tract XC (1841). Although his interpretations were largely repudiated at the time, many of them have become commonplace in later Anglo-Catholic interpretation of the Articles.[6]

The acceptance of the historical critical method in 19th century Anglicanism was cautious and gradual. Landmarks in this development are: the Colenso affair (1861-3), *Essays* and Reviews (1869) and *Lux Mundi* (1889), which opened up the acceptance of biblical criticism to many in the Tractarian school . . . Tractarianism and Broad churchmanship thus combined to loosen Anglican attachment to the Articles and therefore to the supremacy of Scripture.

The first official result of this loosening of the attachment to the Articles was the relaxing of the terms of subscription at Ordination in the Church of England.[7] Prior to 1865 every Minister at his ordination, institution or licensing had to accept the Thirty-nine Articles, the Book of Common Prayer and the Ordinal *ex animo*.[8] Now, in the rewording of the declaration and subscription this is altered as follows:

I, A.B., do solemnly make the following declaration: I assent to the Thirty-nine Articles of Religion, and to the Book of Common Prayer, and the Ordering of Bishops, Priests and Deacons; I believe the Doctrine of the . . . Church of England . . . as therein set forth, to be agreeable to the Word of God.

It would seem from this that the Articles are no longer to be regarded as they were in Archbishop Laud's time, as the basic hermeneutical instrument for the interpretation of Scripture. They are on their way to becoming what they are now in many branches of the Anglican Communion — including this one — relegated to the status of historical documents of the past.[9]

The second major quasi-official pronouncement of the 19th century was the Report of the Lambeth Conference of 1888. This is chiefly famous for the Chicago-Lambeth Quadrilateral. This formula spoke of four elements in a sacred deposit as a basis of approach toward what the Lambeth bishops referred to as "Home Reunion," namely, Scripture, the Apostles' and Nicene Creeds, the two Gospel sacraments and the historic Episcopate. It placed Holy Scripture first, thus recognizing its primary; it quoted Article VI in saying, speaking of Scripture, "as containing all things necessary to salvation," and further defined them as the "rule and ultimate standard of faith." This is a recognition of its supremacy.

But there was another less known but equally important statement to emerge at Lambeth, 1888, and this is perhaps the last attempt to produce an authoritative or quasi-authoritative statement of the bases of Anglican faith. This is the report on "Authoritative Standards of Doctrine and Worship."

This states the common faith that holds the Churches of the Anglican Communion together.[10] It speaks of the one faith revealed in Holy Writ, defined in the Creeds, maintained by the primitive Church and affirmed by the undisputed Ecumenical Councils. Of Holy Scripture it says that we recognize with the general consent of the Fathers, that the canonical Scriptures of the Old and New Testaments "contain all things necessary to salvation," and are the rule and ultimate standard of all Christian doctrine. It goes on to say that the Anglican Church accepts the Creeds, including the *Quicunque vult,* whether recited in public worship or not (was this strictly true of the American Church, which at that time never mentioned this Creed in its Prayer Book or Articles?). The Creeds are said to rest upon certain warrant of Scripture. They define the fundamental mysteries of the Trinity and Incarnation, thus guarding believers from lapsing into heresy (*sic!*). In regard to the Councils, it states that the Anglican Churches have always recognized the first four on matters of faith and that there is no point of dogma in which they disagree with the 5th and 6th, but that the 7th

Council (Nicea II) deals only with the (to us) irrelevant and non-doctrinal question of ikons.

In the second section of the report the bishops turn from the standards of the Universal Church to the local standards which are the peculiar heritage of the Church of England and which are received by all her sister and daughter Churches to a greater or lesser extent. These are the Book of Common Prayer, including the Catechism and Ordinal, and the Thirty-nine Articles.

Several comments on this important and largely forgotten statement of Lambeth 1888 are called for. First, the Scriptures are given a central and normative role in matters of faith. Second, in the phrase that we recognize the supreme authority and centrality of Scripture "with the general consent of the Fathers" the bishops of 1888 set Holy Scripture in the context of Tradition. But this tradition is carefully specified. The Nicene Creed as a Creed of the Universal Church is given priority, and the Apostles and Athanasian Creeds are recognized as purely Western, though congruent with Scripture. As noted, what these Creeds really yield is the doctrine of the Incarnation and the Trinity. It is these, in the last analysis, which provide for classical Anglicanism the hermeneutical key to the interpretation of Scripture.

The Articles are even more local: properly they are the peculiar heritage of the Church of England. This is how the statement is elaborated:

> With regard to the 39 Articles of Religion we thank God for the wisdom which guided our fathers, in difficult times, in framing statements of doctrine, for the most part accurate in their language and moderate in their definitions . . . At the same time we feel that the Articles are not all of equal value, and do not profess to be a complete statement of Christian doctrine, and that from the temporary and local circumstances under which they were composed, they do not always meet the requirements of Churches founded under wholly different circumstances.

They go on to make the interesting point that while they would not recommend requiring the acceptance of the Articles as a condition of "complete inter-communion" (what today we would call "full communion") nevertheless we should expect them — especially when such churches receive from the Anglican Communion their episcopal succession — to furnish satisfactory evidence that they hold substantially "the same type of doctrine with ourselves."

One rub's one's eyes at all this in the light of the more lax attitude towards doctrine manifest in later Anglican official or quasi-official pronouncements. In 1888 Anglicans were insistent that unity of faith was important in keeping the Anglican Communion together, not just episcopacy, or communion with the Archbishop of Canterbury or a common Prayer Book.

It was a little unfortunate that the Lambeth Report of 1888 antedated that domestication of historical critical methods from Germany that took place through the work of Charles Gore and William Sanday. Gore contributed an essay on "The Holy Spirit and Inspiration" in *Lux Mundi* (1889), while in 1893 Sanday delivered the Bampton Lectures under the title of *Inspiration*. Both of them rejected the view that inspiration meant a guarantee of historical inerrancy. Both of them insisted that we should start with the biblical authors as human writers with all the accompanying limitations. Gore in particular anticipated Pope Piux XII's *Divine Afflante Spiritu* (1944) in distinguishing the different literary genres in Scripture. Yet both agree that we find in them inspired truth.

Gore, as an heir of the Tractarians, was able to embrace historical critical methods because for him part of the weight of faith was shifted from Scripture to the Creeds, and the tradition of the undivided Church. But this put limits to his criticism. It was essential to him that the Beloved Disciple should have written the Fourth Gospel, because this work was a major prop for the doctrine of the Incarnation; that St. Luke derived the information for his Infancy Narrative from the Blessed Virgin Mary, because this was an essential prop for the Virgin Birth; and that the Pastorals were authentically Pauline, because this supported the apostolic origin of episcopacy.

The next generation of Liberal Catholics — such people as my own teacher Sir Edwyn Clement Hoskyns, and my own Bishop, A. E. J. Rawlinson — broke with Gore's caution on these matters. These later scholars of the Liberal Catholic School were prepared to accept the critical views about the Lucan infancy narratives (Rawlinson, e.g., called them poetry rather than history); on the Fourth Gospel (not an historical record by an eyewitness but an interpretation of apostolic tradition), and on the Pastoral Epistles (deutero-Pauline). If the traditional Anglican position as laid out in the Quadrilateral was to be maintained it could only be so as the result of a development. Scripture does not set out catholic faith and order in its fullness as a blue print. Rather, it sets in motion certain lines of development which will reach their completion after the New Testament period. It is in this sense that Lambeth 1930 expounded the Quadrilateral:

> The Episcopate occupies a position which is, in the point of historical development, analogous to that of the Canon of Scripture and the Creeds. In the first days there was no Canon of New Testament Scripture, for the books afterwards included in it were still being written. For a time, different churches had different writings which they regarded as authoritative. The Canon was slowly formed, and the acceptance of a single Canon throughout the Church took several generations. So, too, the Apostles' Creed is the result of a process of growth which we can in large measure trace. If the Episcopate, as we find it at the end of the second century, was the result of a like process of adaption and growth, that would be no evidence that it lacked divine authority, but rather that the life of the

101

Spirit within the Church had found it to be the most appropriate organ for the functions it discharged.

This was an updating of the traditional Anglican position that though the authority of Scripture is primary, the exercise of that authority is distributed among secondary authorities, the Canon, Creed, episcopate, Fathers and Councils, and tertiary authorities (the Articles, Lambeth pronouncements, etc.).

This diffused character of the Anglican understanding of authority was further emphasized at Lambeth 1948. In a section of the Report dealing with the nature of authority we read:

> Authority, as inherited by the Anglican Communion from the undivided Church of the early centuries of the Christian era, is single in that it is derived from a single Divine source, and reflects within itself the riches and historicity of the divine revelation, the authority of the eternal Father, the incarnate Son, and the life giving Spirit. It is distributed among Scripture, tradition, creeds, the ministry of the Word and Sacraments, the witness of the saints, and the *consensus fidelium,* which is the continuing experience of the Holy Spirit through his faithful people in the Church. It is thus a dispersed rather than a centralized authority, having many elements which combine, interact with, and check each other.

Several comments are called for here. First, we note that there is a reference here to an authority behind that of Scripture itself, namely the authority inherent in the Tri-une God. This recalls in some ways Barth's positing of an authority of the Word who is the incarnate One behind the word of Scripture. For the event character of revelation is adequately recognized in the reference to historicity.

Second, although Scripture is placed first in the list, it appears only as one secondary authority among others, rather than as the supreme earthly authority and witness to the historical revelation to which all secondary and tertiary authorities must agree (contrast what the Articles said about Creeds and Councils). Primacy remains, supremacy has been abandoned.

Third, one may perhaps welcome the broader definition, "Ministry of Word and Sacraments" rather than episcopacy. But the authority of the Church in "Controversies of faith" (Article XX) is not mentioned. This suggests that the belief that there can be such a heresy which needs to be squarely faced is losing ground. The doctrinal erosion of Anglicanism is already becoming apparent. On the other hand the reference to the witness of the saints and to the *consensus fidelium* is a welcome enrichment. This guards against the older, too static Anglican view which overstressed the role of antiquity, as though the Holy Ghost has ceased to guide us into all truth since the time of the ancient fathers and catholic bishops.

Fourth, there is no reference to the Articles (contrast 1888). Already they are being relegated to the status of historical documents! They disappear with the supremacy of Scripture.

Lambeth 1958 addressed itself explicitly to the Holy Bible: Its Authority and Message. A. M. Ramsey, then Archbishop of York, was the chairman and moving spirit behind the committee which studied this topic and produced the report, and everywhere the influences of "biblical theology" — in its heyday in the 40s and 50s — is at work. The report begins by emphasizing the distance of the Bible from modern throught, what Hoskyns called "the strangeness of the biblical world." And instead of questioning the relevance of the Bible on these grounds (as D. E. Nineham, M. Wiles, J. Nick *et al* would today), the Report sees this strangeness as a judgment on modern thought. It notes the growth of fundamentalism and attributes this to a craving for authority which it believes the biblical theology approach to the Bible can satisfy. It is optimistic about the influence of the biblical message in the contemporary life of the church, pointing to the revival of biblical theology, the liturgical movement, the development of biblical ways of prayer, the concern about the language and thought forms of the biblical message.

The second part of the report deals with the place of the Bible in the Church. It notes that the people preceded the book. But although the Church preceded the Canon, it did not *confer* authority on it, but rather *acknowledged* its authority. The Report goes on to note the change in the concept of inspiration brought about since the 19th century by historical critical method. Previously all the narrative parts of the OT and NT had been taken to be literally true, though the full consequences of this were often in practice circumvented by allegorical interpretation. The Report affirms that the use of the historical critical method is justified because of Christianity's appeal to history. How then can Scripture be understood today as the Word of God? The Report rejects the approach of evolutionary liberalism, which had been adopted in the quasi-official Report of the Archbishop's Commission on Christian Doctrine of 1938 and the talk of "progressive revelation" fashionable before the rise of biblical theology, and instead opts for the biblical theology approach to the Bible as the witness of the "mighty acts of God." The Bible is the word of God because God spoke in the historical events of Israel's history, and in Jesus Christ the Word became flesh. The OT is the witness to those mighty acts in Israel's history, and the NT the apostolic testimony to Jesus Christ. He is central, and the OT and NT are the Word of God because the OT promises His coming and the NT witnesses to the fulfillment of those promises.

This section of the report recognizes that there are other forms of God's word than his mighty acts and the biblical witness to them. For instance, there are propositional statements and moral commands. Biblical inspiration is recognized and defined as testimony to the revelation of God in Israel's history and in Jesus Christ. The Spirit was at work in *all* the books which serve that revelation: any notion of degrees of inspiration is rejected.

The characteristically Anglican diffusion of authority reappears, but with a more explicit insistence on the supremacy and primacy of Scripture than in 1948:

> Such is the pattern of Christian belief. The Creeds summarize it. The Church expounds it in systematic form. But it is from the Bible that every right exposition of it derives.

A warning is issued against radical reinterpretations of the biblical message, which discard certain elements because of their allegedly outdated character. This is a veiled warning against Bultmann's demythologizing program.

The report makes the best statement of preaching I have encountered in any Anglican document:

> The preaching of the Word is far more than teaching

> The preaching of the Word is far more than teaching about the Gospel. It is the means whereby Jesus, who is the Word, becomes vivid to the hearers in his presence, his gift, and his demand.

A final section deals with the moral teaching of the Bible. In the OT this is summed up in the Ten Commandments. Jesus radically reinterprets them and sums up his radical interpretation in the double commandment of love. The moral teaching of the Bible thus becomes not a code but a description of Christian character. The Church from time to time makes moral pronouncements, thus exercising its power of binding and loosing.

This is the fullest — and for me the most congenial — of all Anglican statements on the Bible. But I must admit that I am prejudiced. Like Bishop A. M. Ramsey, I was a pupil of Sir Edwyn Hoskyns, and I am an unrepentant adherent of the biblical theology movement, in spite of all that has happened since 1958.

Let us now turn to the Report of Lambeth 1968, which once more took up the question of authority. It included the following passage:

This inheritance of faith is uniquely shown forth in the Scriptures and proclaimed in the Catholic Creeds set in their context of baptismal profession, patristic reasoning and conciliar decision. These the Anglican Communion shares with other Churches throughout the world. In the sixteenth century the Church of England was led to bear a witness of its own to Christian truth, particularly in its historic formularies — the Thirty-nine Articles of Religion, the Book of Common Prayer, and the Ordinals as well as its Homilies. Together these constitute a second strand in the Anglican tradition. In succeeding years the Anglican Communion has continued and broadened this responsible witness through its preaching and worship, the writings of its scholars and teachers, the lives of its saints and confessors, and the utterances of its councils. In this third strand, as in the Preface to the Prayer Book of 1549, can be discerned the authority given within the Anglican tradition to reason, not least as exercised in historical and philosophical inquiry, as well as the acknowledgement of the claims of pastoral care. To such a threefold inheritance of faith belongs a concept of authority which refuses to insulate itself against the testing of history and the free action of reason.

There is much to be welcomed in this statement. Once more we note the primary and unique place given to Scripture, set in the context of Tradition. And there are some new things, particularly the recognition of a third strand — preaching and worship, the work of scholars and teachers, the lives of saints and confessors, and the utterances of Anglican Councils. This breaks with a constant danger in classical Anglicansim, one which eventually drove Newman to Rome — the *static* character of its attitude to Scripture and antiquity. The recognition of the role of reason, which goes back to Hooker, is now related to historical critical method. But something is missing which is so strongly affirmed by the Articles — the supremacy of Scripture — that Scripture is the criterion of all the other authorities. Indeed, there is an ambiguity about the place given to Scripture. It ranks first and is said to be unique, yet it is classed *with the Creeds* in the group of primary authorities. It would have been truer to the Articles and the classical Anglican tradition if Scripture had been placed by itself apart from the primary, as well as the secondary and tertiary authorities.

Meanwhile the sixties had witnessed the rise of radical theology, beginning, as far as Anglicanism is concerned, with *Soundings,* a volume of essays by Anglican scholars at Cambridge, and edited by Alec Vidler. This was followed by *Honest to God* (1963) and in the American Church by James Pike's *A Time for Christian Candor* (1964). James Barr and others attacked biblical theology and celebrated its demise. The first effect this new stirring had in the Church of England was increasing restlessness over clerical assent to the Thirty-nine Articles. So in 1968 the Doctrinal Commission studied the question and came out with a proposal that His Majesty's Declaration should be dropped from the Articles, that a new Preface should be inserted, modeled closely on the paragraph we quoted from the 1968 Lambeth Report (with both its strengths and weaknesses), and the substitution of these words of assent:

> I, A. B., profess my firm and sincere belief in the faith set forth in the Scriptures and in the Catholic Creeds, and my allegiance to the Doctrine of the Church of England.

These proposals were implemented in the Church of England in 1975. The profession is clearly weaker than that still made in the Protestant Episcopal Church as printed in the 1979 Book of Common Prayer:

> I solemnly declare that I do believe the Holy Scriptures of the Old and New Testaments to be the word of God, and to contain all things necessary to salvation; and I do solemnly engage to conform to the Doctrine, Discipline, and Worship of the Protestant Episcopal Church in the United States of America.

But there has also been doctrinal erosion over here. The Bayne Report of 1967 by the commission set up after the Pike Affair made the following statement:

> We are of the opinion that the word "heresy" should be abandoned except in the context of the radical, creative theological controversies in the early, formative years of Christian Doctrine.

107

Is such a statement consistent with the traditional Anglican assertion of the primacy of Scripture, interpreted in the context of the Creeds etc.? The Report of 1888 had not shrunk from speaking of heresy!

I will here forego an analysis of 1979 *Book of Common Prayer* in the light of scriptural doctrine. It would be a worthwhile exercise to see how far it has been infected by the doctrinal erosion of the 60s and 70s. Here the collects would be particularly worth investigation.

Instead I will turn to another doctrinal report of the Church of England, *Christian Believing,* issued in 1976 by the doctrinal commission under the chairmanship of Professor Maurice Wiles. Its terms of reference were "The Nature of the Christian Faith and its expression in Holy Scripture and Creeds." The opening section is entitled: "The Adventure (!) of Faith." Christian life, it says, is an adventure, a voyage of discovery, a journey. It says nothing of the Church having an eternal gospel to proclaim, and nothing of the faith once delivered to the saints. The next chapter is entitled The Pastness of the Past. This title clearly comes from Dennis Nineham,[11] who has used it in his recent writings about the cultural conditionedness of the Bible. The Report states, as Nineham has done, that the present age is more distant culturally from the Bible than every other age including the Reformation. It is therefore a very real problem what, if anything, of the Bible can be made to speak relevantly for Christian believing today. There follows next a chapter on religious language. Chapter 4 is devoted to the Bible. It approaches the Bible as a "source" for individual believing. It is entirely unconcerned with the question of the Church's proclamation, which never enters its purview — no doubt this is largely due to the terms of reference, which were focused on what the individual can or should believe. It catalogues the results of biblical criticism. First, there is the great chronological spread of the biblical writings — from before BC to *c.* AD 150. Second, there are the successive cultures which provided the matrix of these writings. Third, there follows a brief historical review of the interpretation of the Bible from the formation of the Canon through the critical movement since 1780. It then reviews the two main post-critical interpretations of the Bible, progressive revelation (cf., the Doctrinal Report of 1938) and the biblical theology movement (cf., Lambeth 1958). Today this second position is no longer tenable. Biblical theology substituted a theology for the Bible itself, and biblical theology obscured the pluriformity of the biblical writings. The Commission writes as though it would really like to get rid of the Bible, but unfortunately we are stuck with it! So the Bible must be kept because it is the beginning of the tradition we have to wrestle with. But it is with the whole of the tradition we have to wrestle in order to know what we are to believe today. The Bible is a part, a very important part of that tradition, but not the decisive part to which all acceptable tradition must conform.

The fifth and final chapter of the report deals with the Creeds. Creeds, it notes, are unique to Christianity. They are formulated to define the saving faith on which the Scriptures converged. But they are not very satisfactory today. They were formulated in the light of current controversies, and pick up different things from those we would pick out today, e.g., they say nothing about the Eucharist and little about the Holy Spirit. Where necessary they used nonbiblical language (e.g., homoousios) and moreover that is not the language we would use today. The Commission notes four different attitudes toward the Creeds among people in the Church of England today:

1. For some the Creeds are the indispensable criterion for all current statements of faith.
2. There are those who have reservations about some features, e.g., the Virgin Birth, but continue to use the Creeds because they unite

109

us with the past and with ecumenical Christendom today.

3. The Creeds belong irretrievably to the past, and therefore many are unhappy with their continuing use.

4. There are those for whom Christianity is a life rather than the holding of a series of *crendenda*.

In a typically Anglican way, the commission ends up by saying that all these points of view contain elements of truth and should therefore be held in tension.

It should be remembered that this report was concerned with individual belief and that it is largely descriptive. It is not concerned with the Church's faith or with its proclamation. But it prompts the description of contemporary Anglicanism as one of disintegration and erosion. It is no wonder that an Anglican theologian has recently written a book entitled *The Integrity of Anglicanism,*[12] and asks whether we have not lost it. It is certainly a marked contrast to the Thirty-nine Articles, the Lambeth Report of 1888 and that of 1958.

But lest we conclude on such a pessimistic note, let us point to two recent signs of recognition of the old Anglican view of the supremacy of Scripture and of the importance of tradition as the context for its interpretation. The first is *An Agreed Statement on Authority in the Church* (Venice, (1967), put forth in that year by the Anglican/Roman Catholic International Commission (ARCIC):

Through the gift of the Spirit the apostolic community came to recognize in the words and deeds of Jesus the saving activity of God and their mission to proclaim to all men the good news of salvation. Therefore they preached Jesus through whom God has spoken finally to men. Assisted by the Holy Spirit they transmitted what they had heard and seen of the life and words of jesus and their interpretations of his redeeming work. Consequently the inspired documents on which this is related came to be accepted by the Church as a normative record of the authentic foundation of the faith. To these the Church has recourse for the inspiration of its life and mission; to these the Church refers its teaching and practice. Through these written words the authority of the Word of God is conveyed. Entrusted with these documents, the Christian community is enabled by the Holy Spirit to live out the Gospel and to be led into all truth.

After this opening statement on the primacy and supremacy of Scripture, the Venice document treats at length the secondary authorities — the Creeds and Councils, the bishops and the question and problem of a primacy among the bishops. All in all, the Venice document seems true to the authentic Anglican tradition of recognizing the primacy and supremacy of Scripture and the diffusion of its exercise among secondary and tertiary authorities whose authority is legitimate so long as what they proclaim is consonant with the primary authority of Scripture.

The second document is the *Moscow Statement Agreed by the Anglican-Orthodox Joint Doctrinal Commission 1976* (London: SPCK, 1977). Section II of this statement is entitled "The Inspiration and Authority of Holy Scripture." It contains the following statement:

> The books of Scripture contained in the Canon are authoritative because they truly convey the authentic revelation of God, which the Church recognized in them. Their authority is not determined by any particular theories concerning the authorship of these books in the historical circumstances in which they are written. The Church gives attention to the results of scholarly research concerning the Bible from whatever quarter they may come, but it tests them in the light of its experience and understanding of the faith as a whole.

Section III, entitled "Scripture and Tradition" rejects the view that these are twin sources of revelation. Scripture is the "main criterion to test traditions to see whether they are out of the Holy Tradition." Holy Tradition "completes" Holy Scripture only in the sense that it safeguards the integrity of the biblical message. Holy Tradition is expressed in dogmatic teaching, liturgy, discipline and spiritual life. Section IV deals with the authority of the Councils. The latter maintain the biblical witness and provide an authoriative interpretation of it. The Anglican members state that Anglicanism is accustomed to lay more emphasis on the first four Councils, although they

111

have no quarrel with the dogmatic decrees of the 5th, 6th, and 7th. They suggest that this problem could be solved by the Vatican II notion of the hierarchy of truths.

Some of the language here sounds odd to Anglican ears (e.g., the term "Holy Tradition") — but when it is all spelled out it seems to accord with the traditional Anglican view of the diffusion of the practical exercise of the primary authority of Scripture. But is it entirely satisfactory on the supremacy of Scripture? It is when it comes to speak of tests of scholarly research and traditions that it falls short of the uncompromising *sola scriptura* of the Thirty-nine Articles. Scripture is the "main" test, no the sole test of tradition, and the test of scholarly research is not Scripture but the Church's experience and understanding of the faith as a whole.

I quote these two quasi-official sources, not because their statements are free from problems, but because they do something to redress the impression one gets from other recent Anglican statements which suggest an abandonment of the traditional Anglican view on the supremacy of Scripture, and its use as the sole criterion for the secondary and tertiary authorities among which its practical exercise is diffused. For the Articles the secondary and tertiary authorities are acceptable only where "they may be proved by the most certain warrants of Holy Scripture."

NOTES

1. For the Ten Articles and other documents of the Henrician Reformation see H. Gee and W.J. Hardy, *Documents Illustrative of English Church History* (London: Macmillan, 1896).
2. See Lambeth 1888 and the Moscow Statements, both discussed below. Cf. also C. B. Moss, *The Christian Faith* (London: SPCK, 1943), who makes the surprising statement that "The six Oecumenical Councils have always been accepted by the Church of England." He cites only individual authorities in support of this claim.
3. See the claim made by R. C. P. Hanson, "A Marginal Note on Comprehensiveness," *Theology* 75 (1972), 635: "All Anglicans are united in accepting the dogmatic tradition of the Church up to 451."

4. On "His Majesty's Declaration" see the Note on p. 18 of *Subscription and Assent to the 39 Articles* (London: SPCK, 1968).

5. Such was the interpretation of the late Bishop G. K. A. Bell of Chichester, and of the late Professor Norman Sykes (from personal recollection of conversation).

6. See e.g., E. J. Bicknell, *A Theological Introduction to the Thirty-nine Articles* (3rd ed. rev. by H. J. Carpenter, London and New York: Longmans, 1955). Many of Newman's interpretations were anticipated in Gallican and other accommodating Roman Catholic interpretations of the Articles in the 17th and 18th centuries.

7. See the report, *Subscription and Assent*, p. 11.

8. *Ibid.*

9. *Book of Common Prayer*, 1979, p. 863 ff.

10. For an account of this report see A. M. Allchin, "Unity of Faith: the Anglican View," *Sobornost* 4/9 (1963) 492-99. He informs us that the Committee responsible for this report included two first-rate scholars, John Wordsworth, Bishop of Salisbury, and John Dowden, Bishop of Edinburgh.

11. E. g., Dennis E. Nineham, *The Use and Abuse of the Bible* (London: Macmillan, 1967) and *idem., Explorations in Theology* (London: SCM, 1977).

12. Stephen W. Sykes, *The Integrity of Anglicanism* (London: Mowbray, 1978).

The Doctrine of Word and Scripture in Luther and Lutheranism
by Robert J. Goeser

There is presently a polarization in American Luther-anism over the understanding of Word and Scripture. It is not new to its history, and in the twentieth century there have been shifts in the form of the polarization. Although the task of this paper attends to one pole of interpretation, the other must be referred to as well. Let us distinguish them most quickly in this way: the one pole (or interpretation) is determined by Luther and the confessions, the other is determined by Lutheran scholasticism of the seventeenth century.

Luther's understanding of the Word of God is among the most creative and complex elements of his theology.[1] His grasp of the Word pervades his restructuring of theology (his 'reading of Christianity') at every point. It does so organically and not just as the first article of his theology. I use three terms as an exposition of his views: *sola scriptura,* Biblical interpretation, and the concept of Word itself.

Luther's reformation understanding of Word and Scripture did not begin with a formal principle of the authority of Scripture; still less did it begin with a particular theory of inspiration. The formal principle was preceded by a creative new understanding of the Word and a complex new way of interpreting Scripture. The principle of *sola scriptura* came at the end of this development.

Sola scriptura as a formal principle must be examined first in the historical setting of the struggle over the form of tradition and its relation to Scripture in the Middle Ages. In the early Church, tradition was the inclusive term to express — and to assure — the continuity of the Church with the total revelatory event in which the life, teachings, death, and resurrection of Jesus the Christ cohered. Scripture and tradition were a part of the same continuity. The late medieval concern, however, was authority and not continuity. There was no method of evaluating traditions historically, and extreme claims were sometimes made: claims of post-apostolic revelations, equal in authority to the Scripture, whose validity was to be judged by the papacy; claims of an oral tradition — preserved by the hierarchy—going back to the words of Jesus and the apostles, with authority equal to the New Testament. These materials could not be subjected to public scrutiny, not be examined historically. Direct and blunt also were the claims of papacy or council to have authority above that of the Scriptures.[2]

Luther's response was to limit normative revelation to the written word; esoteric oral tradition was excluded. The revelatory documents are subject to historical examination. *Sola scriptura* presupposes the clarity of Scripture; its literal meaning and its meaning for salvation are clear. The hierarchy does not have power over interpretation because of the hiddenness of Biblical language. Luther also studied church history in terms of development; tradition could no longer be viewed a-historically.[3]

The authority of Scripture rests neither on historical judgment nor on external theories of inspiration, but always on the Word. Word and Scripture are to be distinguished according to Luther. Word is at once more inclusive than Scripture and is expressed as person, event, or proclamation; as written, it is record of these. It is Word which is means of grace. The Word bears God's revealed presence. It is Word which authenticates Scripture, makes it authoritiative, and it is authoritative insofar as it bears the Word.

Luther gave various concrete expressions to this relation between Word and Scripture. Scripture is authoritative for example, because of its capacity to become oral Word, proclamation, address. Scripture and spoken Word are distinguished, and yet the authority of Scripture presupposes its potential spokenness, its potential addressness. It is as if Scripture becomes itself through the spoken Word, which makes out of the past revelatory encounters recorded in Scripture a contemporary event, makes revelation "available", of use to the heart.[4] The translatability into contemporary event by the spoken word constitutes Scripture's authority. Scripture is the record of a Word proclaimed; it is the record of revelational encounters. It is the bridge between past revelatory events and their contemporary renewal as revelation. Revelation can become revelation only as new encounter and not as historical transcription.

That *sola scriptura* refers to content is, in fact, well enough known from the many and sometimes charmingly worded passages that Christ is the heart or center of the Scriptures. What would be left, if Christ were taken from the Scriptures? (Tolle Christum e scripturis, quid amplius in illis invenies?")[5] Christ may be pitted against the Scriptures. Christ stands for the whole meaning of promise, where promise is at once grounded in creation, history, and present encounter, and also stands for the opposite of the law which is fallen man's religion and a fundamental perversion of creation.

The hermeneutical shift accomplished by Luther is a qualified break with traditional allegorical interpretation, the development of an evangelical interpretation, and an affirmation of the clarity of Scripture. Luther recognized that allegory developed on the soil of Platonic dualism; as such, he saw that the created, the natural, was endangered. The concreteness of reality in its created, temporal forms was made to be second-rate, inferior to timeless abstractions. Luther insists that the richness and variedness of the concreteness and historicalness of the created must not be reduced to a reflection of eternal ideas.[6] The natural must be allowed to stand for what it is, not dissipated allegorically into some disembodied spirituality, nor sublimated into something Christological.[7]

As Luther holds to the concreteness of the created, so he maintains the historicality of event. His approach to the Old Testament reflects well the shift from allegory to event. Medieval interpretation saw the Old Testament as shadow or prefiguration; revelation and grace were only prefigured. The Old Testament consisted either of a past history no longer significant or of anticipatory types which would be fulfilled in the New Testament or in the church. Luther broke with the idea of prefiguration. The

Old Testament is a book of real events of Word and faith. There is real encounter with God's revelatory presence. There is real proclamation and real event. God's Word and work are here present.[8]

Disclosing of event is of a piece with Luther's peculiar ability to open up the humanness of Old Testament stories. All the emotion, conflict, and anxiety are heightened. The story is not an illustration of timeless truth; it occurred in all its concrete humanness. In the Abraham-Isaac story, for example, Luther takes us over the ground to Mt. Moriah. He allows us to evade no suffering, no anxiety, no human emotion. The goal is not imitation of Moses, but a presentation of what it is to live through the present — i.e. the reality of human event.[9]

Luther's turn from allegory meant giving up the traditional four-fold interpretation of Scripture in favor of the grammatical or literal historical meaning of the text. "Faith must be built on the basis of history, and we ought to stay with it alone and not so easily slip into allegories."[10] The history spoken of here is two-fold. On the one hand it is the literal meaning to be probed by the linguistic historical method; on the other hand, it is that historical which is not mere fact, but is able to be appropriated only in faith. The literal meaning itself as revolution involves promise of Christ. This meaning is available only as the proclamation of law and gospel — a proclamation to a hearer-reader who is himself embedded in history and creation. Consequently the proclamation comes as an event. An evangelical interpretation of Scripture is not just message of comfort. Instead, it discerns that the revelatory event of Scripture is not law, teaching, or historical fact (all apprehensible by the intellect); it is a past become contemporary event as address of law and gospel to be appropriated only by the heart in faith.

Luther's Biblical interpretation was identical neither

with Renaissance humanist scholarship nor with modern Biblical scholarship. Nonetheless, his interpretation is possible — at least, so he said — only with the development of humanistic historical, linguistic, and literary tools. The very appeal to the original text represents the insistence that revelation is mediated through documents subject to public historical scrutiny.[11]

Our discussion of the authority and interpretation of Scripture has turned repeatedly on the meaning of Word. It is necessary to discuss the Word separately starting with the recognition that the Word is more inclusive than Scripture in Luther's understanding of revelation.

Most frequently Word means the proclamation, the spoken Word, which embodies God's whole gracious action. Hence, it can refer — by extension — to the whole free proclamation of grace which for Luther constitutes the revival of the Word or gospel in his day.

In this regard, Luther remarks repeatedly in bold language that the gospel is properly a spoken word. For the gospel to be gospel it needs to be spoken, addressed to a you. Ideally the gospel ought never to have been written down. Writing takes away the address character, the character or revelation as event.[12] Historical circumstances forced the writing down of the Gospel in the New Testament. Such a position makes clear that the Word precedes the written Scripture; the Word (gospel) is the determinative principle of interpretation, and Scripture gains its authority from the Word. It is the Word, for example, not the Scripture, which calls the Church into existence.

The Word of address invites and calls for a response. Communication is not completed without response, and the response is of the heart — in modern terms the whole, responsible self. The Word can never be the conveyance primarily of information, facts, teachings, ideas, or law — which then would be received by the intellect or applied in external action.

It is the Word which brings a person before God, *coram deo.* Life *coram deo* constitutes the movement from all objectivity and detachment to the fullest degree of involvement. In Old Testament imagery, Word is that which moves David from behind the judge's bench to the position at the bar being judged. Word thus achieves the most radical level of involvement, responsibility, selfhood.

Here a new view of Word and grace are being articulated. The Word has become the means of grace,[13] yes, but more significantly, grace is no longer understood in terms of substance (and in relation to merit), but in terms of word itself — i.e. language, communication. Word is an encounter with person bringing the self into true historical existence.

A particular function of Word (gospel) is to mediate past revelatory events. The way they become present is through the Word. Luther pours scorn on mere historical or doctrinal faith which would avoid the total commitment which faith represents. The events do not become present *for me* as historical facts, but only as an address which calls forth commitment or faith. No revelatory event can become present except to faith, and the Word makes the event of use to the heart, in faith. This means that I never get beyond the faith situation in receiving revelation. So the resurrection cannot be known as revelation simply as a fact. It becomes of use to me only through the Word, or promise. To know the resurrected Lord is not to know an empirical historical fact; it is to trust that Lord in a life where the outcome cannot be known in advance.

Consequently, revelation can never be subject to empirical verification. It is never available to the senses. (The Word-faith context can never be evaded). I can never see God's revelatory presence with the naked eye, and this for two reasons: first, because faith is a way of knowing which involves the whole self in commitment in time, and second, because sin resists God's way of coming to me. This latter means that revelation is not esoteric, but that it runs directly counter to the values of the old man. So Luther maintains that God's Word is always attached to something created, something physical, but His presence is not empirically perceived.[14] That is, God's revelatory presence can be seen only where there is a death and resurrection. There is no other way according to Luther. Any other way is magic. So miracles, for example, are evident only to the eyes of faith, i.e., to the one being transformed by the Word.

If God's Word is always tied to something physical or created then we can see that revelation is never merely verbal for Luther. The physical or created here stands for the whole historical-created realm. Here is where I hear the Word and where I respond in faith. Word and faith are never an escape from history and creation. We could say that both Word and faith are clothed in the created and the historical. The encounter with revelation moves me into creation and history, not out of them. Surely this represents a very incarnational view of faith and an incarnational-sacramental view of revelation.

Luther ascribes such significance to the preached Word because it is the Word which brings about the reality of the new creation which is faith. The Word destroys, brings to death, the whole distorted existence where man is turned in upon himself, insulated from reality and trying to be in control, not of creation, but of a world of his own making via the law. Man has turned from promise to a world he seeks to control by a law which is a way of salvation. The Word comes as law to destroy the way of the law, to bring to death, and out of the ashes of the old man to bring forth life — the Word of promise or gospel.

Word may be described as bearing Christ's presence. "Again, I preach the gospel of Christ into your heart, so that you may form him within yourself. If now you truly believe, so that your heart lays hold of the Word and holds fast within it that voice, tell me what you have in your heart? You must answer that you have the true Christ, not that he sits here, as one sits on a chair, but as he is at the right hand of the Father."[15] Thus Word bears — not information, not concepts — but the full reality of Christ as he is at the right hand of the Father.

Finally, it is fundamental to observe that the Word is Christ, is the second person of the Trinity. The Word is the living Word of the living God. It is understood after the analogy of human speech (address) and not in terms of the rational principle of the *logos* of the ancient church.[16] The significance of the Word in relation to the trinity could be expressed in the following way. All that Luther means by God's presence in history is summarized in the term Word. Word is communication, but not mere verbalization; it is communication clothed in history and creation.

The Confessions

The Lutheran Confessions do not have the richness, understandably, of Luther's complex and creative presentation of the Word; neither do they give formulae summarizing the doctrine of Scripture in regard to authority and interpretation. There is no article on Scripture, as such, in the Augsburg Confession, the Apology, or the Smalkald Articles. Only in the latest of the confessions, the Formula of Concord (1577), is there anything that could be so called, and it is marked more by brevity than by inclusive or explicit definition:

> We believe, teach, and confess that the prophetic and apostolic writings of the Old and New Testament are the only rule and norm according to which all doctrine and teachers alike must be appraised and judged.

In this way the distinction between the Holy Scripture of the Old and New Testaments and all other writings is maintained, and Holy Scripture remains the only judge, rule, and norm according to which as the only touchstone all doctrine should and must be understood and judged.[17]

The absence of an article on Scripture in the Lutheran Confessions is the more remarkable in view of the articles on Scripture in the Reformed Confessions. In all the early major Reformed confessions (First Helvetic (1536), Second Helvetic (1566), French Confession (1559) and the Belgic Confession (1561), there is a series of articles on Scripture at the very beginning of the confession. They assert the primacy, sufficiency and clarity of Scripture, but they give no explicit theory of inspiration.[18]

These articles on Scripture underscore, by comparison, the absence of such statements in the Lutheran Confessions. Elert sees it as evidence of the avoidance of any biblicism in early Lutheranism.[19] What we know of Luther's view of Word and Scripture from the corpus of his writings must be, of course, the hermeneutical context for understanding these matters in the two catechisms and the Smalkald Articles. The understanding of Word and Scripture in the Augsburg Confession and the Apology does not differ markedly from what has already been written (despite theological difference between Melanchthon and Luther). Word refers to the oral, proclaimed Word, to the re-expressed gospel of grace, to the promise; the gospel is the key to the interpretation of Scripture; Scripture is the record of the Word and authoritative in relation to church and traditon.

The Forumula of Concord is not significantly an exception to the earlier confessions. The statement on the Scriptures is to establish its authority in relation to tradition. Moreover, positions on major issues are determined by long quotations from Luther, and Luther's thought is declared to be the true interpretation of the Augsburg Confession.

Elert summarizes the confessional position by arguing that the final authority of Scripture rests with the soteriological significance of Scripture (Christ, the Gospel) not with a formalistic 'Scripture principle'. The gracious efficacy of the Word is achieved by the connection between Word and Spirit; the efficacy does not rest with a theory of inspiration of Scripture.[20]

Lutheran Orthodoxy

Lutheran orthodoxy presents a very different picture of Word and Scripture from that in early Lutheranism. It is creating a theology of the Word also, but with great differences. Perhaps the most remarkable difference is the loss in orthodoxy of any awareness of the essential character of Word as the spoken Word. Ebeling writes: "It is symptomatic of the impoverishment of the understanding of the Word in orthodoxy that those insights were completely lost from sight. It was no longer borne in mind that to the essence of the Word belongs its oral character, i.e., its character of an event in personal relationship, that the Word is thus no isolated bearer of meaning, but an event that effects something and aims at something."[21] What was lost was not just the oral character. What was not recognized was that proclamation establishes the gracious, relational, event character of Word — that Word always comes as address, encounter, and therefore, as event. Ebeling goes on to say, "The orthodox understanding of the *verbum Dei* as *verbum scriptum* stood on its own in isolation from the proclamation that is to take place, and so shrunk to an unhistoric understanding of Word."[22]

The Word is always the written Word. Word and Scripture are equated. Revelation is defined in terms of the written Word. This position is fundamental both to orthodoxy's understanding of Word and of its way of doing theology.

The equation of Word and Scripture demanded a theory of inspiration as the external, objective validation of the written Word.[23] Scripture is verified not by the Word which is efficacious of faith through the Spirit (not, that is, by a Word which is self-authenticating, because the Word bears the Spirit), but by a theory which is external to the Scriptures' own intrinsic meaning and witness. This theory is now elaborated into a theory of verbal inspiration. Certainty could be ascribed to the written Word only if every word were directly inspired by the Holy Spirit. Hollaz wrote: "There are contained in Scripture historical, chronological, genealogical, astronomical, natural-historical, and political matters, which although the knowledge of them is not actually necessary to salvation are nevertheless divinely revealed . . ."[24] Elsewhere he wrote: "For the prophets and apostles were not at liberty to clothe the divine meaning in such words as they might of their own accord select; but it was their duty to adhere to, and depend upon, the oral dictation of the Holy Spirit . . ."[25] Calov, a major architect of the theory, said succinctly, "No error, even in unimportant matters, no defect of memory, not to say untruth, can have any place in all the Holy Scriptures."[26]

The theory of verbal inspiration was the basis of doing theology in orthodoxy. For example, in Gerhard's great *Loci,* an elaborate and extended doctrine of Scriptures is the first article; on it the whole system was built. Revelation has become propositional truths to be received by the intellect, and theology is a rationalistic method of applying the texts to the whole scheme of knowledge of God and salvation.[27]

American Lutheranism

If this account were to be more complete, some attention would need to be given to developments in the time of Pietism, of Rationalism, and of the emergence of modern theology from the time of Schleiermacher. Instead we turn directly to the American Lutheran scene of the second half of the nineteenth century. Dominant nearly everywhere was the repristination theology (from Germany) which sought to resist modern theological thought and the historical study of the Scriptures by a return to seventeenth century dogmatic theology and its doctrine of verbal inspiration. This theology especially dominated the thought of the churches developing from the new immigration, but it was influential among Lutherans in the East, rooted in the colonial tradition. Krauth, the most influential theologian of the General Council, for example, was open to the thought of some "mediating" German theologians and conservative Erlangen theologians; his work on the American translation committee for revision of the King James version was praised by Schaff; as professor of philosophy at the University of Pennsylvania he was not totally resistant to modern thought — yet he assumed the identification of Word and Scripture and he opposed the new historical scholarship.

This same tradition of eastern, more Americanized Lutheranism, however, by the end of the century and in the next decades did begin to evince positive response to the new Biblical scholarship and some awareness of the creativity of Luther's thought. The progress is slow as evidenced by the doctrinal basis from the constitution of the newly merged United Lutheran Church (1918).

> The United Lutheran Church in America receives and holds the canonical Scriptures of the Old and New Testaments as the inspired Word of God, and as the only infallible rule and standard of faith and practice, according to which all doctrines and teachers are to be judged.

Verbal inspiration is not here explicitly affirmed; yet it is a very conservative statement and could be interpreted in terms of inerrancy. Two years later, however, in the Washington Declaration, verbal inspiration was clearly not assumed, and the following was affirmed: ". . . that in the Holy Scriptures we have a permanent and authoritative record of apostolic truth which is the ground of Christian faith."[28]

In the next decade, theologians of the U.L.C.A., led especially by C. M. Jacobs, developed a theology of the Word of God which recovered many of the insights of Luther and the confessions in contradistinction to the position of Lutheran orthodoxy and repristination theology. It was, above all, the new German Luther research which began to open up the richness of Luther's understanding of the Word.

This theology assumed a clear distinction between Word and Scripture. When the confessions and Luther speak of the Word of God as the means of grace, it is Christ, the Gospel, which is meant.[29] The Word as grace is a person, an event, a proclamation. It is God's activity in history; it is not propositional truths nor inerrantly inspired words. Scripture gains its authority from the Word of which it is a record; revelation is not dependent on a theory of inspiration of Scripture. This understanding owed more to Luther and the confessions than to modern Biblical scholarship, although it was in no way violated by historical study. This view of revelation was in no sense a capitulation to modern thought, not an erosion forced upon theology by modern science. It was understood to be an expression of the very genius of Luther and the confessions.

A good official expression of these views is present in the following statement of the U.L.C.A. — from the Baltimore Declaration of 1938 — formulated largely by Jacobs.

> Both in the Scriptures and in the Confessions of the Church, this term 'Word of God' is used in more than one sense . . . it is important that we should understand what these different senses are and who we mean when we call the Scriptures by this name.
> We believe that, in its most real sense, the Word of God is the

126

Gospel, i.e., the message concerning Jesus Christ, His Life, His Word, His teaching, His sufferings and death, His resurrection and ascension for our sakes, and the saving love of God thus made manifest in Him.

We believe that in and through this Gospel the Holy Spirit comes to men, awakening and strengthening their faith, and leading them into lives of holiness . . . For this reason we call the Word of God, or the Gospel a means of grace . . .

We believe that in a wider sense, the Word of God is that revelation of Himself which began at the beginning of human history, continued throughout the ages, and reached its fullness and completion in the life and work of Jesus Christ our Lord . . .

We believe that the whole revelation of God to men which reached completion in Christ . . ., is faithfully recorded and preserved in the Holy Scriptures through which alone it comes to us. We, therefore, accept the Scriptures as the infallible truth of God in all matters that pertain to His revelation and our salvation.

We believe that as God's revelation is one and has its center in Jesus Christ, so the Scriptures are a unity, centering in the same Lord Jesus Christ. Therefore, we believe that the whole body of the Scriptures in all its parts is the Word of God.

The Scriptures have their more important and their less important parts, and the measure of their importance must always be the closeness of their relation to Christ, our Lord, and to the Gospel, which is the Word of God in the most real sense. . . .[30]

From this statement the distance is not far theologically to the doctrinal basis of the constitution of the Lutheran Church in America (1962). What stands between the two documents is a much more extensive and committed practice of historical Biblical scholarship in the church and also influences from the development of Biblical Theology, the understanding of salvation history, as well as the new hermeneutic — all those developments described so well in Reginald Fuller's paper. From the hermeneutic emerged a sense of the distinctive character of Biblical language and communication and hence of the hermeneutical task. From the Biblical Theology came an understanding of revelation which distinguishes clearly between factual account and revelatory event. Revelation is to be equated neither with the verbal narrative nor with scientific history. It belongs to another realm than that of empirical evidence. It is an event which demands the response of faith and can be seen only by faith; it is an event in the dynamic of a community of faith in history. (The record, of course, is subject to study by exact historical method). The following statement from the L.C.A. constitution clearly reflects this Biblical Theology, as well as Luther's understanding of the Word.

> This church confesses Jesus Christ as Lord of the Church. The Holy Spirit creates and sustains the Church through the Gospel and thereby unites believers with their Lord and with one another in the fellowship of faith.
>
> This church holds that the Gospel is the revelation of God's sovereign will and saving grace in Jesus Christ. In Him, the Word Incarnate, God imparts Himself to men.
>
> This church acknowledges the Holy Scriptures as the norm for the faith and life of the Church. The Holy Scriptures are the divinely inspired record of God's redemptive act in Christ, for which the Old Testament prepared the way and which the New Testament proclaims. In the continuation of this proclamation in the Church, God still speaks through the Holy Scriptures and realizes His redemptive purpose generation after generation.
>
> (Article II, Section 1-3)
>
> This church affirms that the Gospel transmitted by the Holy Scriptures, to which the creeds and confessions bear witness, is the true treasure of the Church, the substance of its proclamation, and the basis of its unity and continuity. The Holy Spirit uses the proclamation of the Gospel and the administration of the Sacraments to create and sustain Christian faith and fellowship. As this occurs, the Church fulfills its divine mission and purpose.
>
> (Article II, Section 7)

The primacy of Christ, the gospel is explicit. By extension revelation includes God's whole redemptive activity in history from creation. Scripture is the record of the revelation. Through the gospel God's revelatory presence continues in the life of the people of God. Revelation is dynamic, not static; it is encounter, not right doctrine.

The doctrinal development just described may be made clearer by contrast with the line of development in the opposite pole of interpretation: the one rooted in Lutheran orthodoxy and repristination theology. Its most

128

consistent formulation is in the theology of the Missouri Synod. Its doctrine of Scripture was first defined by Walther, whose theology was drawn from the seventeenth century dogmaticians. He equated Word and Scripture, insisted that every word of Scripture was directly inspired; if any detail of Scripture were not true the whole of Scripture would be jeopardized and lost. He knew and deplored the rejection of verbal inspiration in much nineteenth century German theology; he was distressed that the rejection was by conservative theologians also. For all his literalism, Walther's real concern was with the gracious efficacy of the Word. The Word as gospel brings the saving knowledge of Christ. The scriptural word when preached is life-giving.[31]

In his *Christliche Dogmatik* (1917-1924) Pieper constructed both the dogmatic position for the Missouri Synod, and defined exactly its doctrine of Scripture. The *Dogmatik* begins with the doctrine of Scripture and builds its system upon it. A doctrine of inerrancy is fully articulated and presented as the view of Luther and the confessions. For Pieper, this doctrine was the defense against modern errors.[32]

This position was re-affirmed officially in the famous *Brief Statement* of 1932. This statement began with the following paragraph on the Scriptures.

> We teach that the Holy Scriptures differ from all other books in the world in that they are the Word of God . . . because the holy men of God who wrote the Scriptures wrote only that which the Holy Ghost communicated to them by inspiration . . . We teach also that the verbal inspiration of Scriptures is not a so-called "theological deduction", but that it is taught by direct statements of Scriptures . . . Since the Holy Scriptures are the Word of God, it goes without saying that they contain no errors or contradictions, but that they are in all their parts and words the infallible truth, also in those parts which treat on historical, geographical, and other secular matters.[33]

These same views have been re-asserted in the struggle over the changing theological position of the Concordia Seminary faculty in St. Louis. This theory of inspiration should not obscure the fundamental hermeneutical and proclamatory concern with the gracious efficacy of the Word and of Christ as the center of Scripture which is also Missouri's position.

In the decades between the wars, the churches which have merged into the American Lutheran Church were also committed to the doctrine of Scripture rooted in orthodoxy. That position has changed and the present theological leadership of the A.L.C. would hold to views of Word and Scripture derived from Luther, the confessions, and contemporary Biblical theology.

Clearly the understanding of Word and Scripture set forth in this paper is one that has been articulated neither primarily to apply historical method to the study of the Scripture, nor to capitulate to modern thought. What is determinative is an understanding of Word and revelation which seems to embody just what is distinctive in the Biblical way of looking at things. It is such an understanding of Word and faith which are true to the uniqueness of the Biblical perspective and keep it from falling into bad philosophy ("send rate Platonism for the masses" in the words of any early critic).[34]

The Word is the word of the Trinity: it is the ground of creation in creation's rational and responsive structures, and still more significantly it is God's gracious, revelatory presence in history at constant work, recreating, in struggle against distortion of creation. This is not an absolute or abstract God, but a God coming always in ways appropriate to the uniqueness of the divine and the human. The presence is incarnational, whether in the history of Israel, most fully in Christ, or through the gospel-event. The response is always in the whole of individuals and the community in the world. Incarnational means that it is always two natured; it is always under human, historical, created forms. Two natured also must be the Scripture which is the record of the classical revelatory events. And so the Scripture is subject to appropriate linguistics, literary, and historical understanding. Anything less would betray incarnation and creation alike.

It is the Word which is the treasure of the church — and its awful responsibility.

NOTES

1. Despite this significance there are few monographs on this topic. The best single work is still Heinrich Bornkamm, *Das Wort Gottes bei Luther* (Munchen 1933). Elsewhere one must look especially to the fine recent studies on Luther's hermeneutics.
2. For documentation of this material see George H. Tavard, *Holy Writ or Holy Church* (London, 1959).
3. John Headley writes, "Never again could there be an unconscious possession of tradition." *Luther's View of Church History* (New Haven, 1963) p. 74.
4. See the comment by Heinrich Beisser: "Wie stark, wie ausschliesslich Luthers Vorstellung von der Heiligen Schrift am gesprochenen Wort orientiert ist, das zeigt sich auf Schritt und Tritt. . . . Diese Auffasjung Luthers ist in ihrer Bedeutung gar nicht zu uberschätzen. Sie impliziert nämlich, dass die Botshaft nich lediglich festliegt, sondern vor allen innerhalb einer lebendigen Beziehung an mich ergeht. . . . Die konkrete Wirklichkeit des verbum externum hat diesen Charakter der Mündlichkeit." *Claritas Scripturae bei Martin Luther* (Gottingen, 1966) p. 85.
5. W. A. 18, 606:29.
6. Martin Luther, *Works* (St. Louis, 1958) Vol. 1, pp. 3-50, and Luther *Works* (Philadelphia, 1974) Vol. 52, pp. 41-88. This could be developed at some length. Luther not only recovers the natural in the Old Testament, he is able to use the Hebrew understanding of creation to oppose dualistic interpretations of New Testament passages. Alongside Luther's "Paulinizing", we may speak of a "Hebraizing".
7. Endel Kallas demonstrates this by a comparison of Luther's interpretation of Ecclesiastes with the earlier exegetical tradition, *Ecclesiastes: Traditum et Fides Evangelica* (unpubl. PhD dissertation, Graduate Theological Union, 1979).
8. See especially James S. Preus, *From Shadow to Promise* (Cambridge, 1969). For medieval Biblical interpretation, see the standard works of Smalley, Spicq, and de Lubac.
9. Luther, *Works,* (St. Louis, 1964) Vol. 4, pp. 91-135.

10. Luther, *Works,* (St. Louis, 1969) Vol. 16, p. 327.

11. The development of Luther's hermeneutics may be placed in the context of university reform, with its concern for the study of languages, history, mathematics, and science. This reform makes clear that Luther's view of Word and Scriptures is not a withdrawal from contemporary thought. See Karl Bauer, *Die Wittenberg Universitats theologie und die Anfänge der deutschen Reformation* (Tubingen, 1928).

12. This is stated frequently by Luther; e.g. Luther, *Works,* Vol. 30, p. 3; W. A. 10[1a] 625-628, W. A. 10[1a] 17-18, and W. A. 10[1b] 34-35.

13. Ernst Bizer, *Fides ex Auditu* (Neukirchen, 1958), and Richard Grützmacher, *Wort und Geist,* (Leipzig, 1902).

14. See, for example, *Against the Heavenly Prophets* (1525), *That These Words of Christ* etc. (1527), and a remarkable sermon on the visitation.

15. Luther *Works,* Vol. 36, p. 346.

16. Luther can also understand the Word in relation to the rational principle (the Logos). See especially the sermons on John.

17. T. G. Tappert, tr. and ed. *Book of Concord* (Philadelphia, 1959) pp. 464-5.

18. Philip, Schaff, Ed., *The Creeds of Christendom,* Vol. III, pp. 211-389, (New York, 1919).

19. Werner Elert observed that the absence of a doctrine of Scriptures was lamented by conservative Lutheran theologians in the nineteenth century. He remarks further that the presence of an article on the Scriptures in the Copenhagen Articles of 1530 argues to a self-conscious omission in the major Lutheran Confessions. *The Structure of Lutheranism* (St. Louis, 1962) Vol. I, pp. 181-187.

20. *Ibid.,* p. 181.

21. Gerhard Ebeling, *Word and Faith* (Philadelphia, 1963) p. 313.

22. *Ibid.*

23. For the orthodox view of Word and Scripture, see Robert Preus, *The Inspiration of Scripture* (Mankato, 1955).

24. Heinrich Schmid *The Doctrinal Theology of the Lutheran Church* tr. Hay and Jacobs (Philadelphia 1899) p. 46

25. *Ibid.,* p. 47

26. *Ibid.,* p. 49

27. For the structure of the orthodox systems, see Hans E. Weber, *Reformation, Orthodie und Rationalismus,* parts I and II (Darmstadt, 1966) and Robert Preus, *The Theology of Post Reformation Lutheranism,* 2 vol. (St. Louis, 1970).

28. Richard Wolf, *Documents of Lutheran Unity in America* (Philadelphia, 1966), p. 348.

29. In ALC — ULCA discussions on Word and Scriptures, Jacobs

wrote: "The Word of God is the Gospel . . . The Augsburg Confession says the means of Grace is the Gospel . . . When we talk about the Word of God, then, we mean Christ, we mean the Gospel. Take Luther's Introduction to the Romans, what is the word of God? The Gospel . . ." Jacobs then goes on to derive inspiration of Scripture from the prior category of Word. Quoted in E. Clifford Nelson, *Lutheranism in North America 1914 - 1970* (Minneapolis, 1972), p. 102. See also Jacobs' inaugural address as president of Philadelphia Seminary. (*Lutheran Church Review,* vol. 46 (1927), pp. 207-225)

30. Wolf, *op. cit.,* pp. 357-8.
31. Carl Meyer, "Walther's Theology of the Word" in *Concordia Theological Monthly,* vol. 43 (1972), pp. 262-283.
32. Franz Pieper, *Christian Dogmatics* (St. Louis, 1950) vol. I, p. v.
33. Wolf, *op. cit.,* pp. 381-2.
34. It is surely significant that when a shift in the attitude toward Scripture was first introduced to Concordia Seminary in papers by Martin Sharlemann, that he started from the kind of view of Word and revelation derived from Luther, the confessions, and Biblical theology much like that of C. M. Jacobs. Note the following quotations from Sharlemann:

> What the sacred writers record and what they give their witness to is God's faithfulness in keeping His promises. They do so, moreover, from within their own personal limitations in terms of historical, geographical, or scientific information. Luther could, therefore, remark that the author of Kings was more accurate than the writer of Chronicles in his historical statements.

> In the first place it (inerrancy) obscures the nature of Biblical revelation; for it is the term used on the level of observation and factual precision. But this notion of truth is not found in the Scriptures. Moreover, using the term 'inerrancy' suggests that the primary concern of the Bible is to furnish information of some sort or another.

> The very limitations of the individual authors in terms of language, geographical, historical, and literary knowledge testify to the specifics of divine revelation. This is part of the 'Scandal of the Bible'. An insistence on its inerrancy is often an attempt to remove this obstacle. The use of this term invariably results in a docetic view of the Bible — and so tends to overlook that our Sacred Scriptures are both human and divine documents.

> Strictly speaking and in a primary sense, the Scriptures are not in themselves a revelation. Our Bible is the record of God's revelatory acts.

The Biblical documents confront us . . . with personal testimony, with an interpretation of events. This is not without its bearing on the art of Biblical interpretation. The working and formulations of the Scriptures almost always intend to point beyond themselves to the great events of what we have called *Heilsgeschicht*. They cannot be handled adequately by a methodology bound to a two-dimensional approach of occurrence as mere fact.

These quotations are given in David Owren, *The Doctrine of Inerrancy of Scripture in the Theology of the Lutheran Church-Missouri Synod* (unpubl. ThM Thesis, Pacific Lutheran Theological Seminary, 1977), pp. 81-114.

Part III
Earlier Dialogues

Recommendations From the
Lutheran-Episcopal Dialogue, Series I

The first series of Lutheran-Episcopal Dialogues were held from 1969 to 1972 under the co-chairmanship of the Reverend O.V. Anderson (LCA) and the Right Reverend Richard S.M. Emrich, Episcopal Bishop of Michigan. As part of its report the participants adopted the following specific *recommendations:*

I. Recognition of agreement between Lutherans and Episcopalians on the following fundamentals of church life and doctrine:

    a. The primacy and authority of the Holy Scriptures

    b. The doctrine of the Apostles' and Nicene Creeds

    c. Justification by grace through faith as affirmed by both the Lutheran Confessions and the Anglican *Book of Common Prayer* and Thirty-Nine Articles of Religion

    d. The doctrine and practice of Baptism

    e. Fundamental agreement on the Holy Eucharist, through with some differences in emphasis:

II. Agreement that our two communions have maintained the essential apostolicity of the church . . .

III. Subject to the consent of the appropriate local authorities (the ordinary or those responsible for recognizing and furthering agreement in the preaching of the Gospel and the ministration of the Sacraments):

Commendation of communicants of each communion

to the Eucharistic celebrations and gatherings around the Word of the other, including intercommunion between parishes or congregations which, by reason of proximity, joint community concerns, and/or activities, have developed such a degree of understanding and trust as would make intercommunion an appropriate response to the Gospel.

IV. As requisite accompaniments of the above, the creation of such structures as will enable Episcopalians and Lutherans, within their new fellowship, to assume joint responsibility for the proclamation of the Gospel with one accord and for an appropriate ministration of the Sacraments, these to include:

A. Continuing joint theological study and conversation, at a level similar to that of the conversations just concluded, with such arrangements for broad discussion as will assure influence on the thought and practice of both communions. Topics for these discussions would include:

1. Continuing concentration on the nature of the Gospel and its effective proclamation,

2. Exploration of future common forms of ordered ministry and *episcopē,* and

3. To further the continual reform and renewal of the church, close study of such features of the sacramental practices of our respective communions as may obscure or distort their character as Gospel, and

B. Participation of consultants from each communion in all deliberations of the other touching sacramental order or confessional status.

Enabling Legislation

In the interests of facilitating the above steps, we respectfully urge our respective communions to enact, as soon as may be feasible, such legislation, canonical or otherwise, as may be required.

Report of the International
Anglican-Lutheran Conversations
(The Pullach Report)

Authorized by the Lambeth Conference and the Lutheran World Federation. The full report from which the following excerpts are taken, is published in *Lutheran-Episcopal Dialogue,* Cincinnati, Forward Movement Publications, 1972.

On behalf of the participants in the recent Anglican-Lutheran Conversations, we submit the following report for the attention of the authorities which commissioned us. Our report is unanimous. The Commission owed much to its secretaries Canon Robert M. Jeffery and the Rev. Michael Moore and especially to Dr. Günther Gassmann who was responsible for much of the final drafting.

I. Introduction

(1) In spite of occasional contacts and a common awareness of great areas of affinity of doctrine, worship, and church life, Anglican and Lutheran Churches have in the past lived largely in separation and in relative isolation from one another. One painful manifestation of their separate existence has been the absence of *communio in sacris* between Lutheran and Anglican Churches (apart from that enabled by regulations concerning different grades of intercommunion between the Church of England and various Scandinavian Lutheran churches).

(2) A new situation has been created by more frequent encounters in recent times, both between churches and individual members of the two communions; the recognition of new, converging tendencies in their biblical and theological thinking; the realization of their common task of mission and service in the modern world; more frequent but still responsible acts of intercommunion;

and the encounter of Lutheran and Anglican Churches in union negotiations.

* * *

(9) After four meetings (at Oxford, September 1970; Løgumkloster, Denmark, March-April 1971; Lantana; Florida, January 1972; and Munich, April 1972) our group completed its work insofar as it was possible in the time given to us. We submit our report including its recommendations to our respective authorities. We are aware of its limitations. We have not attempted to say everything that should or could be said in common.

(10) We have attempted to articulate lines of thought which are already accepted in much of the past and present thinking of our churches. This implies that we tried to be as representative as possible of the traditions and present developments in our churches. We hope that the articulation of current tendencies may itself advance and extend our ecumenical unity.

* * *

II. Theological Considerations

A. Sources of Authority

a) Scripture

(17) The Anglican and the Lutheran Churches hold that it is Jesus Christ, God and Man, born, crucified, risen, and ascended for the salvation of mankind, in whom all Scriptures find their focus and fulfilment. They are at one in accepting the Holy Scriptures of the Old and New Testaments as the sufficient, inspired, and authoritative record and witness, prophetic and apostolic, to God's revelation in Jesus Christ.

(18) Both churches hold that through the proclamation of the gospel and the administration of the sacraments, based on the same Scriptures and empowered by the Holy Spirit, Christ is speaking to us and is active amongst us today, calling us to live and serve in his name.

(19) Both churches hold that nothing should be preached, taught or ordered in the church which contradicts the word of God as it is proclaimed in Holy Scripture.

(20) Within both churches different attitudes exist concerning the nature of inspiration and the ways and means of interpreting the Scriptures, and these attitudes run across the denominational boundaries.

(21) Both churches agree in stressing the need and responsibility for a continuing interpretation of the biblical texts in order to communicate the gospel of salvation to all men in different times and changing circumstances.

(22) They teach that the whole church, and especially the ministry of the church, has received the responsibility for guarding all proclamation and interpretation from error by guiding, admonishing and judging and by formulating doctrinal statements, the biblical witness always being the final authority and court of appeal.

b) *Creeds*

(23) The Anglican and the Lutheran Churches are at one in accepting offically the Apostles' and Nicene Creeds. These creeds are used regularly in their worship and in their teaching. They recognize the Athanasian Creed as giving a true exposition of the trinitarian faith.

(24) They believe that these creeds are authoritative summaries and safeguards of the Christian faith. Their authority is established in the first place by their faithful witness and interpretation of the biblical message, and in the second place by their acceptance and use in the Early Church. They, therefore, hold a unique place among all confessional documents.

(25) The acceptance of these creeds implies agreement between both Communions on the fundamental trinitarian and christological dogmas.

c) Confessional formularies

(26) The Lutheran and the Anglican Churches developed and accepted a number of confessional documents at the time of the Reformation. There are a great number of direct historical and theological connections and similarities between these documents.

(27) They did not regard these confessions as "foundation documents" of a new church, but rather as means of safeguarding and witnessing to the faith of the church at all times.

(28) They regarded these confessions as expositions of their final authority, namely Holy Scripture. The confessions were aimed at a renewal and reformation of the church making it as inclusive as possible, but guarding against certain errors and misguided developments in late medieval Roman Catholicism on the one hand, and against "enthusiastic" and extreme movements on the other.

(29) On the Lutheran side the confessions of the Reformation still occupy officially a prominent place in theological thinking and training, in catechetical teaching, in the constitutions of the individual Lutheran churches and at the ordination of pastors. They serve as a link between the churches of the Lutheran family.

(30) On the Anglican side the 39 Articles are universally recognized as expressing a significant phase in a formative period of Anglican thought and life. The significance attached to them today in Anglican circles varies between Anglican churches and between groups within Anglican churches. On the other hand the Book of Common Prayer has for a long time served as a confessional document in a liturgical setting. Though liturgical revisions vary among Anglican churches, the influence of the Prayer Book tradition is still evident.

(31) Since confessional formularies are not a mark of the church their significance lies in their expression of the

living confession to the living Lord. Different approaches to the authority of these formularies are possible between Communions so long as they share a living confession which is a faithful response to the living word of God as proclaimed in Holy Scripture.

d) *Tradition*

(32) The Anglican and the Lutheran Churches are at one in regarding tradition as a normal element in the life of the church.

(33) By the word "tradition" is meant the way in which the apostolic witness (i.e. "tradition") has been transmitted from one generation to the next, from one culture to the other. By the word "traditions" are meant the ways in which the churches have developed their thinking, worship, common life, and attitudes to the world.

(34) Both churches agree that all traditions are secondary to tradition and that they, therefore, have to be tested by that tradition. If they are in accordance with, and expressions of, this ultimate standard they are to be regarded as important means of continuity. In order to serve this purpose they should never become petrified, but remain open for change and renewal.

(35) The attitude toward the tradition, especially over against the tradition of the Early Church has found within both churches different expressions at different times and in different schools of thought.

(36) Anglicans do not make frequent use of the word "tradition" except in a phrase like churches of the Anglican tradition, which is virtually a synonym for the "Anglican Communion." But during a Reformation period (which for Anglicans extended from 1534 to 1662) they called on the teaching of the Early Fathers in their apologies against both Roman Catholics and Puritans.

(37) A positive appreciation of the patristic tradition, already apparent in the sixteenth century, became more marked in the seventeenth, and made its influence felt in

141

Anglican spirituality, ecclesiology, and liturgy — the Scottish liturgy of 1637 is an example of this. The Oxford Movement of the nineteenth century saw a further phase in the appropriation of both patristic and medieval traditions and a new sense of the unbroken continuity of the church's history.

(38) At all times, however, there has been a sharply critical attitude to tradition if this implied an additional source for historical data supplementing the history given in the gospels, or a source for a "secret" doctrine additional to that given in the scriptural witness.

* * *

(44) Modern scholarship (Exegesis, Patristics) has in many ways served as a means of convergence between different denominations. This also applies to and has consequences for our evaluation of early tradition. But even if there remain a number of different emphases in this field, they are certainly not of fundamental importance, but rather expressions of different histories, ways of thinking and life, which should be a source of mutual enrichment and correction.

e) *Theology*

(45) Within the Anglican and the Lutheran Churches the position, function, and character of theology have developed in a number of different ways.

(46) Both communions stress the importance of theological reasoning and both look back to a rich tradition of theological work.

* * *

(49) Both communions, therefore, are much more closely connected in the field of theology today than ever before. Part of this closer relation grows out of the fact that they face the same problems and tensions within their theological thinking.

(50) Thus, remaining marked differences in the function and emphasis of theology should be welcomed as an expression and sign of a legitimate variety within the one people of God.

B. *The Church*

(51) The Anglican and the Lutheran Churches adhere to the traditional Nicene characterization of the church as *one, holy, catholic, and apostolic,* and they believe that they are expressions of this church. This position was reaffirmed by each church at the Reformation and has been continuously maintained as a specific definition of what the church is called to be in the world.

* * *

(53) Both traditions agree that the *unity* of the church, God's gift and our task, must be manifested in a visible way. This unity can be expressed in different forms depending upon the particular situation. Accordingly there can be various stages in the mutual recognition of churches, in the practice of intercommunion and in the reciprocal acceptance of ministries. The goal should be full "altar and pulpit fellowship" (full communion), including its acceptance by the individual members of the churches, and structures that will encourage such fellowship and its acceptance.

(54) The two traditions confess with one accord the *holiness* of the church as a gift of God's grace separating the church to himself as a beloved and forgiven people, which by the power of his Spirit is inspired and called to a life and mission which reflects among men God's own holiness. Within each tradition and between the traditions there have been and are differences of emphasis and interpretation concerning the practical expression of this holiness in the church's life and mission. Such differences are not mutually exclusive and need not prove divisive in the life of the church.

(55) In maintaining the *catholicity* of the church, Anglicans and Lutherans confess together, that the fullness of the truth of the gospel is committed to the church. Further, they recognize together the universal outreach and inclusiveness of the church, extending to every nation, race and social group. Finally, they seek to comprehend the wholeness of human life in all its aspects under the dominion of Christ. Both churches, however, are aware of the danger of particularist claims within their denominations. "Catholic fullness" and "the pure doctrine of the gospel" may be misinterpreted to present the exclusive privilege of particular groups or parties. Fullness, universality, and wholeness belong only to the one body of Christ.

(56) In the concept of *apostolicity* there is common ground insofar as all teaching, life and ministry of the church have to be in continuity with the fundamental apostolic witness and commission to go out into the world. It is the role which the succession of bishops plays within this wider concept of apostolicity which is one of the main controversial points between the two traditions. Consequently section D. in this report will consider the apostolic nature of the church and its ministry.

* * *

(58) As the people of God growing out of the Old Covenant, the church lives in the New Covenant and is sent by Christ to serve mankind. As the Body of Christ, the church lives in an intimate relationship with him, the head of the Body. Despite its frailty and failures, it is sustained by the faithfulness of its Lord. At the same time, the church is constantly built up, renewed and strengthened by Christ's actual presence and action, through Word and Sacrament, in the Holy Spirit.

(59) The church, therefore, is the recipient of grace, a community and royal priesthood of the people of God

responding to this gift in corporate praise and thanksgiving to God, and responding simultaneously as an instrument for proclaiming and manifesting God's sovereign rule and saving grace. Because the church is sent into the world to continue Christ's service and to witness to his presence among all mankind in liberating men from fear and false idols, in meeting human need, and in fighting against injustice and discrimination, the nature and mission of the church belong inseparably together. Mission and service presuppose an authentic fellowship of the reconciled. A fellowship without mission is disobedient to the commandment of its Lord.

60) The fellowship of the church calls for a deep mutual sharing of the spiritual and material gifts of God. Being a fellowship of those who are at once sinful in themselves but made righteous in Christ, the church is, nevertheless, a first fruit of the kingdom and, therefore, it prophetically witnesses to the final joy of mankind which is to lose itself in wonder, love and praise of the Creator, Redeemer, and Sanctifier. So the church is a pilgrim people, exposed to God's judgment and nourished on its way by his grace which exceeds both our achievements and our desires or deserts.

C. The Word and the Sacraments
a) Relation of Word and Sacrament

(61) Both our communions affirm in virtually the same words (Conf. Aug. VII, XIX) that the right proclamation of the Word and the proper administration of the sacraments are essential and constitutive to the ongoing life of the church. Where these things happen, there we see the church.

(62) To be obedient to the will of Christ the church must honor both Word and Sacrament and must avoid emphasizing one to the neglect of the other.

(63) While there is some difference in the mode of

Christ's action in Word and Sacrament, both Word and Sacrament are occasions of his coming in anamnesis of his first advent and in anticipation of his parousia. The Word imparts significance to the sacrament and the sacrament gives visible embodiment to the Word.

b) Baptism

(64) Baptism, administered with water and the threefold name, is the effective means by which God brings a person into the covenant of salvation wrought by Christ and translates him from darkness and bondage into the light and freedom of the kingdom of God. The baptized are grafted into the church, adopted as children of God, brought into a relation with him which means justification, the forgiveness of sins and exposure to the sanctifying power of the Holy Spirit in the believing, witnessing, and serving community.

(65) Faith is necessary for the right receiving of the sacrament. Infant baptism, though not certainly attested in the New Testament, is conformable to its doctrine and in particular to the emphasis on the divine initiative in man's redemption. The faith of the parents, sponsors and the whole community, is a pledge that the baptized infant will be brought to respond in faith to what God did for him in baptism.

(66) The practice of infant baptism necessitates the provision of opportunity for personal profession of faith before the congregation. In both our traditions this has been associated with confirmation in which the bishop (in Anglicanism) lays hands upon the candidate or the parish pastor (in Lutheranism) lays hands upon the candidate or otherwise blesses him. We note the debate within each communion about precise aspects of the theology and practice of confirmation, including its relation to admission to communion. Since the points so debated cut across the denominational lines, they ought not to be

barriers to communion between us.

c) The Lord's Supper

(67) In the Lord's Supper the church obediently performs the acts commanded by Christ in the New Testament, who took bread and wine, gave thanks, broke the bread and distributed the bread and wine. The church receives in this way the body and blood of Christ, crucified and risen, and in him the forgiveness of sins and all other benefits of his passion.

(68) Both communions affirm the real presence of Christ in this sacrament, but neither seeks to define precisely how this happens. In the eucharistic action (including consecration[1]) and reception, the bread and wine, while remaining bread and wine, become the means whereby Christ is truly present and gives himself to the communicants.

[1] i.e., the setting apart of the elements, the recitation of the thanksgiving with the words of institution, and the invocation of the Holy Spirit, whether explicit in the liturgical words or not.

(69) Both traditions affirm that Christ's sacrifice was offered once and for all for the sin of the whole world. Yet without denying this fundamental truth both would recognize that the Eucharist in some sense involves sacrifice. In it we offer our praise and thanksgiving, ourselves and all that we are, and make before God the memorial of Christ's sacrifice. Christ's redemptive act becomes present for our participation. Many Anglicans and some Lutherans believe that in the Eucharist the church's offering of itself is caught up into this one offering. Other Anglicans and many Lutherans do not employ the concept of sacrifice in this way.

d) Of the number of the sacraments

(70) Both our traditions recognize the uniqueness of the two gospel sacraments. Of these alone is there in the New Testament a recorded command of Christ to perform specific actions with material things, and to these alone is

attached a specific promise to his own action and gift annexed thereto.

(71) In both communions there are those who would extend the term sacrament to other rites (e.g., absolution and ordination among Lutherans, and the other five of the traditional "sacraments" by Anglicans). This is largely a matter of nomenclature. Under the stricter definition there can be others, but when the wider definition is used the preeminence of Baptism and the Lord's Supper is still maintained.

(72) Within both communions some provision is made for the other "five commonly called sacraments" according to need and local variation. Where unction is practised it is not understood as extreme unction but as a means of healing.

D. Apostolic Ministry
a) Apostolicity and apostolic succession

(73) The apostolocity of the church is God's gift in Christ to the church through the apostles' preaching, their celebration of the gospel sacraments, and their fellowship and oversight. It is also God's sending of the church into all the world to make disciples of all nations in and through the apostolic gospel. Thus apostolicity pertains first to the gospel and then to the ministry of Word and sacraments, all given by the risen Lord to the apostles and through them to the church. Apostolicity requires obedience to the original and fundamental apostolic witness by reinterpretation to meet the needs of each new situation.

(74) The succession of apostolicity through time is guarded and given contemporary expression in and through a wide variety of means, activities, and institutions: the canon of Scriptures, creeds, confessional writings, liturgies, and activities of preaching, teaching, celebrating the sacraments and ordaining and using a

ministry of Word and Sacrament, the exercising of pastoral care and oversight, the common life of the church, and the engagement in mission to and for the world.

b) The ministry

(75) In confessing the apostolic faith as a community, all baptized and believing Christians are the apostolic church and stand in the succession of apostolic faith. The apostolic ministry which was instituted by God through Jesus Christ in the sending of the apostles is shared in varying ways by the members of the whole body.

(76) The ordained ministry of Word and Sacraments is essentially one, though it assumes a diversity of forms which have varied from New Testament times, and which still vary according to local conditions and historic influences down to the present.

(77) We feel ourselves called to recognize that all who have been called and ordained to the ministry of Word and Sacrament in obedience to the apostolic faith stand together in the apostolic succession of office.

(78) It is God who calls, ordains, and sends the ministers of Word and Sacrament in the church. He does this through the whole people, acting by means of those who have been given authority so to act in the name of God and of the whole church. Ordination to the ministry gives authority to preach the gospel and administer the sacraments according to Christ's command and promise, for the purpose of the continuance of the apostolic life and mission of the church. Ordination includes the prayer of all the people and the laying on of hands of other ministers, especially of those who occupy a ministry of oversight and unity in the church.

c) Episcopacy

(79) "Episcope" or oversight concerning the purity of apostolic doctrine, the ordination of ministries, and

pastoral care of the church is inherent in the apostolic character of the church's life, mission and ministry. This has been embodied and exercised in the church in a wide variety of forms, episcopal and non-episcopal. Both Communions have continuously held and exercised oversight in accordance with their respective understanding of church order.

(80) In the Lutheran Communion episcopacy has been preserved in some parts in unbroken succession, in other parts in succession of office, while in other parts oversight has been exercised in non-episcopal forms. In all forms it has experienced the blessings of the ministry in the church.

(81) In the Anglican Communion Episcopacy has been preserved in a succession unbroken at the time of the Reformation and, rightly or wrongly, important deductions have been drawn from this in relation to the organic continuity and unity of the church.

(82) Both communions are open to new forms in which episcope may find expressions appropriate to the needs and conditions of the situation and time.

d) Particular convictions and perspectives of each Communion

Statement of the Anglican participants:

(83) Anglicans treasure the historic episcopate as part of their own history and because of their belief in the incarnational and sacramental character of God's involvement with the world and his people. As God acts now in and through words spoken, in and through bread and wine, and in and through the reality of human community, so too he acts in the laying on of hands in historic succession, providing for the ministry of Word and Sacrament in the one church.

(84) They believe that the episcopacy in historic continuity and succession is a gift of God to the church. It is an

outward and visible sign of the church's continuing unity and apostolic life, mission, and ministry. They hold this belief while recognizing that episcopacy has been and may be abused in the life of the church, as have been the other media of apostolic succession.

(85) Anglicans do not believe that the episcopate in historic succession alone constitutes the apostolic succession of the church or its ministry. The participants wish to declare that they see in the Lutheran Communion true proclamation of the Word and celebration of the sacraments. How we are able to make this statement while maintaining our adherence to the importance of the historic episcopate we hope the Anglican personal note (see section IV) will make clear. The Anglican Communion has been much influenced and blessed by God through the Lutheran Communion's faithfulness to the apostolic gospel. We, therefore, gladly recognize in the Lutheran churches a true communion of Christ's body, possessing a truly apostolic ministry.

(86) Such recognition, if reciprocated by the Lutheran churches, implies, according to the mind of the participants, official encouragement of intercommunion in forms appropriate to local conditions.

(87) The Anglican participants cannot foresee full integration of ministries (full communion) apart from the historic episcopate, but this should in no sense preclude increasing intercommunion between us, which would give fuller and more joyful expression to our unity in Christ, recognize and deepen the similarities which bind us together, and provide the most appropriate context for our common service of the one Lord.

Statement of the Lutheran participants:

(88) The Lutheran churches have practised full fellowship with each other regardless of the forms of episcope (or even of the episcopate). With ecumenical developments

this freedom for fellowship has allowed Lutheran churches to enter into fellowship with non-Lutheran churches with various forms of church government.

(89) Since full fellowship has been retained between some Lutheran churches which have not preserved the office and name of a bishop and other Lutheran churches which have retained the historic episcopate in a form similar to the Anglican and since the particular form of episcope is not a confessional question for Lutherans, the historic episcopate should not become a necessary condition for interchurch relations or church union. On the other hand, those Lutheran churches which have not retained the historic episcopate are free to accept it where it serves the growing unity of the church in obedience to the gospel.

(90) The Lutheran participants in these conversations recognize the churches of the Anglican Communion as true apostolic churches and their ministry as an apostolic ministry in unbroken succession, because they see in them true proclamation of the gospel and right administration of the sacraments. As would be true for any church which proclaims the gospel in its purity and administers the sacraments properly the participants regard the historic episcopacy as it has been retained in the Anglican Communion as an important instrument of the unity of the church.

(91) The Lutheran participants in these conversations recommend to the member churches of the Lutheran World Federation that they work for a still closer fellowship with the churches of the Anglican Communion, including at the present time intercommunion. Where it is expedient for furthering the mission of the church and where it can happen without disturbing already existing relations with other churches, Lutheran churches must be free to manifest a mutual recognition of ministries through the exchange of ministers or through full church union.

E. Worship

(92) Our conversations have given the participants renewed opportunities to enter into each other's traditions of worship and spirituality. Both sides have been impressed with the similarity between their respective heritages of liturgical worship and also with the close similarity between the movements for liturgical reform in both communions. The deep reverence and liturgical care with which their common services of the Eucharist have been conducted remain among the most cherished memories of the experiences which the delegates have gone through together.

* * *

(94) Now, in both churches, the Holy Communion is coming back into the center of the picture as the principal worship service of each Sunday. In the Lutheran churches there is a marked re-appropriation of traditional liturgical forms of worship and in Anglicanism there is a noticeable tendency to reintegrate Word and Sacrament, particularly by the use of the sermon in many more celebrations of the Holy Communion. Both traditions use increasingly spontaneous and informal modes of prayer and praise in the setting of traditional liturgical frameworks.

* * *

III. Recommendations

A. Intercommunion and Fellowship

a) *Intercommunion*

(96) The degree of mutual recognition of the apostolicity and catholicity of our two churches indicated in the report justifies a greatly increased measure of intercommunion between them. Both Anglican and Lutheran Churches should welcome communicants from the other church and should encourage their own communicants to receive Holy Communion in churches of the other tradition where appropriate and subject to the claims of

individual conscience and respect for the discipline of each church.

(97) An anomalous situation exists in Europe. The Church of England should no longer make a distinction in the intercommunion arrangements made for various Lutheran churches, but should extend the arrangements for Sweden and Finland to include all Lutheran churches in Europe. The many years of contact with Sweden and Finland have made a useful introduction to the communion and fellowship which would thus be extended and which should be reciprocal.

b) *Joint worship*

(98) In places where local conditions make this desirable, there should be mutual participation from time to time by entire congregations in the worship and eucharistic celebrations of the other church. Anniversaries and other special occasions provide opportunity for members of the two traditions to share symbolic and ecumenical worship together.

c) *Integration of ministries*

(99) In those countries where Anglican and Lutheran churches are working side by side for the spread of the gospel, or where there are churches with close relationships with our two communions (we have Africa and Asia especially in mind), there is felt a need for more rapid movement towards organic union. We endorse this. It is our hope that our report, with its encouragement of inter-communion and its recognition of the apostolicity of both churches and their ministries, might facilitate progress towards a true integration of ministries. Whatever steps may be taken towards such integration, nothing should call in question the status of existing ministries as true ministries of Word and Sacrament.

* * *

D. Joint Local Mission and Social Witness

a) *Shared facilities and ministries*

(105) In areas where the presence of one or more churches

154

in very small, one ministry might serve more than one communion by incorporating smaller groups into the parish life or larger, although in various ways allowing the smaller groups to remain in touch with their own communions. Isolated clergy of any communion should be welcomed into meetings of clergy of larger churches so that the clergy of many churches might meet as one body. Sharing building and pastoral services may provide good opportunities for mutual service and fellowship.

b) *Social witness and evangelism*

(106) Joint action for mission, social witness, and education is recommended wherever relevant and possible. This might include the interconfessional running of educational institutions such as colleges or schools for the handicapped, and cooperation wherever possible; joint work for the alleviation of illiteracy; joint preparation and publication of Christian literature; and the sharing of facilities on university campuses, for youth centers, and in new industrial areas and housing estates.

c) *Discussion and dialogue*

(107) There should be in all regions some form of continuing interchurch discussions by official joint delegations and local groups on the various ways in which our two traditions may move closer together and on the forms of unity into which God may be calling us. These should include consideration of the theological convictions which may still tend to separate us (e.g., the proclamation of the gospel, the historic episcopate).

(108) It is our hope that our present discussions will have elucidated many of the issues relevant to our relationships. We submit our report in the hope that it may be made available to all our member churches and contribute to closer fellowship among us in Christ our Lord.

Anglican participants:
Bishop R. R. Williams, Leicester, England (Chairman); Prof. J. Atkinson, Sheffield, England; Archdeacon J. A. Cable, Itki, Bihar, India; Prof. W. R. Coleman, Downstown, Canada; Bishop R. S. M. Emrich, Detroit, USA; Prof. R. H. Fuller, New York, USA: Prof. S. L. Greenslade, Oxford, England; Prof. J. R. Rodgers, Alexandria, USA; Bishop N. Russell, Roslin, Edinburgh, Scotland; Canon R. M. Jeffery, London, England (Secretary); Rev. M. Moore, London, England (Secretary).

Lutheran participants:
Archbishop em. G. Hultgren, Uppsala, Sweden (Chairman); Bishop H. H. Harms, Oldenburg, Germany; Prof. B. H. Jackayya, Nagercoil, South India; Bishop J. Kibira, Bukoba, Tanzania; Dr. K. Knutson, Minneapolis, USA; Dr. R. J. Marshall, New York, USA; Prof. R. Prenter, Aarhus, Denmark; Prof. M. Schmidt, Heidelberg, Germany; Dr. G. Gassmann, Strasbourg, France (Secretary).

LWF staff:
Dr. C. H. Mau, Geneva, Switzerland; Dr. P. Højen, Geneva, Switzerland.

WCC:
Prof. N. Robinson, St. Andrews, Scotland (Observer).
April, 1972.

PARTICIPANTS IN THE LUTHERAN-EPISCOPAL DIALOGUE, SERIES II

The American Lutheran Church

Dr. Ralph W. Quere
Wartburg Theological Seminary
Dubuque, Iowa

Dr. Richard L. Trost
Central Lutheran Church
Eugene, Oregon

Dr. Robert L. Wietelmann, *co-chairman*
Good Shepherd Lutheran Church
Kettering, Ohio

American Evangelical Lutheran Church

The Rev. Cyril Wismer, Sr., Auxiliary Bishop
American Evangelical Lutheran Church
Falls Village, Connecticut

Lutheran Church in America

Dr. J. Stephen Bremer
Lutheran Memorial Church
Madison, Wisconsin

Dr. Robert J. Goeser
Pacific Lutheran Theological Seminary
Berkeley, California

The Rev. Frank Senn
Lutheran School of Theology
Chicago, Illinois

Lutheran Church-Missouri Synod

The Rev. Carl L. Bornmann
St. John's Lutheran Church
Luxemburg, Wisconsin

The Rev. Jerald C. Joersz, Ass't. Exec. Secretary
Commission on Theology & Church Relations
St. Louis, Missouri

Dr. Norman E. Nagel
Valparaiso University
Valparaiso, Indiana

Lutheran Council in the U.S.A

Dr. Paul Opsahl 1976-79
Dr. Joseph Burgess 1979-80
Lutheran Council, Division of Theological Studies
New York, New York

Episcopal Church, U.S.A.

The Rev. Reginald H. Fuller
Virginia Theological Seminary
Alexandria, Virginia

The Very Rev. J. Ogden Hoffman, Jr.
Trinity Episcopal Church
Folsom, California

The Rev. William H. Petersen
Nashotah House
Nashotah, Wisconsin

The Rev. J. Howard Rhys
The School of Theology
The University of the South
Sewanee, Tennessee

The Very Rev. John H. Rodgers, Jr.
Trinity Episcopal School for Ministry
Ambridge, Pennsylvania

The Rev. Louis Weil
Nashotah House
Nashotah, Wisconsin

The Rt. Rev. William G. Weinhauer, *co-chairman*
Bishop of Western North Carolina
Black Mountain, North Carolina

Dr. Peter Day 1976-80
The Rev. William A. Norgren 1980
Ecumenical Officer, Episcopal Church Center
New York, New York

For Further Reading

Gritsch, Eric W., and Jenson, Robert W. *Lutheranism.* Philadelphia: Fortress Press, 1976.

Lutheran Book of Worship. Minneapolis: Augsburg Publishing House, and Philadelphia: Board of Publication, Lutheran Church in America, 1978.

Marty, Martin E. *Lutheranism.* Royal Oak, Michigan: Cathedral Publishers, 1975.

Nelson, E. Clifford. *Lutheranism in North America, 1914-1970.* Minneapolis: Augsburg Publishing House, 1972.

Nelson, E. Clifford, ed. *Lutherans in North America.* Philadelphia: Fortress Press, 1975.

Tappert, Theodore G., ed. *The Book of Concord.* Philadelphia: Fortress Press, 1959.

The Book of Common Prayer. New York: The Church Hymnal Corporation and The Seabury Press, 1979.

Neill, Stephen. *Anglicanism.* Harmondsworth, Middlesex: Penguin Books, 1958.

Norris, Richard A. *Understanding the Faith of the Church.* New York: The Seabury Press, 1979.

Sykes, Stephen W. *The Integrity of Anglicanism.* New York: The Seabury Press, 1978.

Wolf, William J., ed. *The Spirit of Anglicanism.* Wilton, Connecticut: Morehouse-Barlow, 1979.

Petersen, William H., and Goeser, Robert. *Traditions Transplanted, The Story of Anglican and Lutheran Churches in America.* Cincinnati, Ohio: Forward Movement Publications, 1981.